Messages from the Coast

Meditations on God's Word

Theodore Allwardt

CreateSpace
an Amazon company

Scriptural references
are taken from
Holy Bible: New International Version
(copyright 1978)

Cover Photo: Secret Beach
Curry County, Oregon

ISBN-13: 978-1501060632

Also written by Theodore Allwardt:

Rattlesnakes and Rainbows:
Daily Devotions Along the Trail of Life

Books, also in Kindle form,
are available on *Amazon.com*

With thanks to the Lord
for using me
to proclaim His message of
forgiveness through Jesus
and
to those who assured me that
He did use my "Messages"
to help them in their
spiritual lives.

CONTENTS

Christian Faith and Living

Grace – Mercy – Peace
Because of Jesus

Grace – God's undeserved love which gives us forgiveness of our sins.

Mercy – God's undeserved kindness which gives us the help we need in the struggles of life.

Peace – God's undeserved blessing which we experience, because we know we are safe spiritually (forgiveness) and physically (His protection and help) as we live day by day until we are with Him forever.

So we can say that grace, mercy, and peace are God's blessings to us spiritually, physically, and emotionally.

But we have none of these except for Jesus, God come to earth, to be our Savior.

This is the perspective from which all my "Messages from the Coast" have been written.

The "Messages" in this book have been selected from the weekly "Message" I continued to write and send out to friends across the country, after I fully retired from the active ministry in 2010. Since a number of these were especially helpful to some who read them, I wondered if I should gather some of the more meaningful ones together for publication. Various friends encouraged me and suggested some they would like included. Most of those included were specifically suggested, but others I decided to include to give a broader selection of Scriptural teachings.

They are divided into two sections: "Church Year and Special Days" and "Christian Faith and Living".

A few of these "Messages" have been preached publicly, but all have been written as though I were preaching them (which is why you will notice so many exclamation points are included). I patterned my preaching style according to how I understand the Apostle Paul preached. His epistles were actually worship service "sermons", since he wrote them to be read and discussed in house-church worship services.

Paul wrote in a conversational style, trying to anticipate the questions that might come to the minds of those who read/heard his message. But especially he not only always included a clear explanation of the Gospel message of Jesus being the Savior, but also he kind of "sprinkled" references to that Gospel here and there in the rest of his message in a very natural way. I like to say that he "breathed" the Gospel in his preaching so that his hearers always remembered to trust in Jesus only and would want to live as thanks to Him. I hope you see this pattern in my "Messages" also.

Since these "Messages" were written over a nearly five-year period, you will notice some repetition of phrases as well as some dated examples. But these "Messages" are not meant to be read like a book with chapters. Rather I urge you to use them as an additional weekly meditation for your spiritual life. You may also want to read specific ones as these might be relevant to what you are facing at particular times on your trail of life.

When you read one, please also read the text it is based

on so you see that I'm not giving you my ideas, but I'm trying to explain and apply His Word for our faith and living. You would probably also find it helpful, I think, to read the suggested "related reading" at that time for more guidance from God's Word.

If you want to use any of these "Messages" as a meditation for a group, you have my permission to do so, although it would be kind if you mentioned the source.

May the Holy Spirit use these "Messages" for your spiritual health, as He has used them to help others as well as the writer.

Grace – mercy – peace – because of Jesus!

Theodore Allwardt

P.S. My special thanks to my wife, Marian, who has been my best listener and encourager for more than 50 years and also has been the proof-reader for my "Messages". Thanks also to my sons, Tim and Ted Allwardt, and to a neighbor, Barbara Wright, for technical assistance and to Liz Crockett of Liz Crockett Design for adapting my photo of Secret Beach for use as the cover photo.

THE CHURCH YEAR
and
SPECIAL DAYS

Theme: **Advent – Our Need**
Related Reading: Luke 1:1-18
Text: Galatians 3:15-20

ADVENT: THE SEED WE NEED

Advent! The word itself essentially means "coming". When I was a kid, I had the idea it meant that Christmas was coming. Later I was taught that it was directing us to think about when He Who came at Christmas was coming again. Thinking back to how this season of Advent came to be, however, I now think that I was more right as a kid than I was after theological training.

To explain: as I understand its history, Advent was begun when in the early centuries of the Christian church, the church leaders decided they needed something religious to help everyday Christians be defended against joining in with the wild orgies which marked the observance of Saturnalia, the winter solstice, when uneducated people then felt assured that life would continue, for the sun had begun to shine a little longer each day after the shortest day of the year. Frankly, Saturnalia was probably just an excuse for excessive immorality and drunkenness, as Marti Gras in New Orleans and Carnival in Rio are today, since surely people's memories were not so short as to doubt that life would go on in a new year, as it always had done. But it became a wide-spread tradition, which new Christians had participated in before coming to faith and which their sinful natures wanted to keep on "enjoying". So, how to help them turn away from such evil activities to live faithful in their trust in Jesus as Savior and Lord?

Some church leaders must have gotten the idea: why don't we celebrate the birthday of Jesus right after Saturnalia and have some weeks of spiritual preparation beforehand? After all, no one knew for sure when Jesus was born (although it may have been in early spring during lambing time, which would be why all the shepherds would be "keeping watch over their flocks at night" instead of merely having them all herded together with only one or two doing the night guarding on a rotation basis – can't be sure, but this may have been the case). Everyone knew when Jesus was crucified and rose – it was at Passover time in the spring, so, let's set the birthday observance enough months ahead of that time so we can kind of review the life of Jesus before His passion and resurrection and Pentecost, 50 days later; then the rest of the year we can instruct our people more fully on Christian teaching and Christian living (we call this now the "Pentecost season").

Therefore, December 25th was chosen as the birth date with four weeks before that date as a time of repentance of sins and of renewed commitment for faithful living. With their minds more focused on spiritual matters, ordinary Christians as well as their leaders would be less tempted to do what all the unbelievers were doing with alcohol and sex. Must have helped, because Advent became a permanent feature of Christian worship life and, after Christianity eventually became the official religion of the Roman world, the Saturnalia excesses at least lessened.

Somewhere along the line the idea then apparently came up: if a birthday, there should be presents, so we will give Jesus our praise for being born and being our Savior, but we will also give gifts to each other. Again, one can't say for sure, but this seems reasonable, from what church history does say, as to how it all worked out. And this is why I think Advent should be thought of primarily as preparing for our celebration of Jesus' birth. Advent! Coming! Jesus' birthday is coming ! Let's get ready, not just physically, but spiritually especially.

Which puts us into the same attitude which Abraham in our text and all the Old Testament people had. God has promised! "All peoples on earth will be blessed through you" (Genesis 12:3) and even more specific: "through your offspring (seed) all nations on earth will be blessed" (Genesis 22:18). Someone is coming! The "Seed" Who will bring blessings from God for all the nations! God has promised! He is coming!

In our text Paul was explaining to the Roman Christians that they could count on being blessed by God, because Jesus had come as God had promised, and had fulfilled God's promises to "save His people from their sins" as the angel had told Joseph (Matthew 1:20). Some false Christians had been claiming that the non-Jews would be saved only if they obeyed all the Old Testament laws. Paul contradicts that idea by saying: but the Law came "430 years later", long after God had established His covenant – and a "covenant" is a legal promise from a more powerful person for the benefit of the less powerful. God's covenant was: I will bless you through this coming One, Abraham's descendant, the "Seed"; but I give this to you free, as long as you accept it on My terms: a gift from Me to you, not a paycheck which you deserve.

Then Paul adds: so, if it was a promised gift, why add the law, that is, not just the Moral Law which had been in effect for all time (example, it has always been wrong to murder) so, not just the Moral Law, summarized in the Ten Commandments, but why add all the other laws and ceremonies which Abraham's primary descendants, the Israelites (descendants through Jacob, Abraham's great-grandson), were to obey? "It was because of transgressions", explains Paul. It was so hard for people to keep waiting century after century for the Promised One to come that the Moral Law didn't seem important so they explained their way around it and took sinning for granted as "no big deal". That's why God added all these extras, meant to be in force only "until the Seed to Whom the promise referred had come". All these extras forced people to admit: I don't do good enough, I sin, I'm a sinner, I need the One Who has been promised to come for blessing. In this way, all these required sacrifices were teaching: you need the real Savior – and He is coming!

All the Old Testament people lived in a kind of Advent attitude – at least they should have: the One is coming! His birth – and His work – are coming!

Advent for us now is: the celebration of His birth is coming, His birth, the act by which He began His work as Savior to bless us with forgiveness of our sins so we have the gift of eternal life. Strictly speaking, of course, His work actually began when He was conceived in Mary's womb – that's when He received humanity into His divine nature so He could be Savior of us humans; but His birth was when His work first became visible.

Jesus is the promised "Seed", the Seed we need, because we are sinners, which the Law, the Moral Law of the Ten Commandments, shows us to be so. The extra laws and requirements of the Old Testament are no longer in force, because it isn't as difficult for us to believe as it was for the Old Testament people. After all, they had to depend on what had not yet happened and over so many centuries with prophecies that were not always very clear. But we look back at the accomplished fact! It still isn't "easy" to believe; but it sure is "easier" to believe the explanation of what actually happened than to wonder about the when and how of what prophets say will happen someday!

Still, we do need the Law, don't we! So easily we think we live pretty good, meaning, do more good than wrong. In fact, how easily we forget the little wrong things we do, the unkind thought, the just slipped out curse word or gossip word, the speed limit we truly broke (more than the extra two miles an hour or so most police allow, instead, really speeding – because everyone else is, aren't they?), the wasted time (not recreation but really wasted on something absolutely meaningless), all these "little" things. And sometimes even "bigger" things: really angry and insulting words, worrying, a lustful desire, refusing to help a neighbor in need, holding a grudge to get even, yes, such things also we can "forget". So, we are pretty good – in our own eyes!

"(The Law) was added because of transgressions": also applies to us. God in effect says: You say "little" – I say sin! You say "pretty good" – I say lost! That's still the purpose of God's Laws: to make us admit our sinning and our lost condition so that we admit our need for the promised Seed, Who did come – for us! For you specifically! For me specifically! He is the Seed we always need, because He is our only way of escape from the punishment we each deserve.

On this first Sunday in Advent we admit our need for Him Who has come. And let's be more specific! Let's each of us, when going to bed each night this week, look back at the day and confess at least one specific sin from that day. And to that confession let us also add: Thank You, Jesus, that You did come – for me! Such a little prayer will help us remain focused on what these December days are truly about: not the piling up of more things (although we can enjoy these also, if we don't overdo them), but truly being thankful for the one Who came into our world so long ago, the Seed Whom we still need every day.   *December 1, 2013*

Theme: **Advent - Prepare**

Related Reading: Luke 1:5-17

Text: Ephesians 3:8-17

ADVENT: THE PREPARING WE DO

So, did you do it? Have the little specific confession of sin each night this past week, as I urged in last week's "Message"? If you did, how did it go for you? Not so easy, was it! At least that was my experience. I found it hard to remember many specific sins of the past day.

Which in a way is as it would be – for a good reason and for a bad reason. The bad reason being: our sinful nature doesn't want to remember – we want to overlook the "little" things! And even the "bigger" things we tend to excuse (he had it coming to him!) or our sinful nature really enjoys them (taking advantage of someone weaker than us to get our way) so we don't "remember" too well.

But a good reason for not remembering the "little" ones is that perhaps there aren't really that many in our day! Which is not being self-righteous, but is merely accepting the reality that God the Holy Spirit does work in us so that we are able to be kind and helpful and courteous in our daily lives. As His children by faith in Jesus, we are able to live more and more as His children should. Which is not a matter of pride for us, but a matter of thanksgiving!

Which probably is why we never feel very guilty when we go to hear the preaching of God's good news: we can honestly say that we are able to live His way reasonably well and we are thankful for being forgiven for whenever we fail. Although there is that other reason for not feeling all that guilty when sitting in the pew (or standing in the pulpit), that sinful pride we at least kind of listen to: not been too bad this past week.

Which is why a preacher must always apply God's law to prick our awareness: oh, oh, that's me – in need of forgiveness always, even when I don't feel guilty. You see, our Christian faith is not built on feelings, neither feelings of guilt nor feelings of awe. Our faith is built on the facts which are explained to us: sinner whether you feel it or not – forgiven because of Jesus whether you feel "faith" or not – but you **know** it! Because God **says** so!

But it is a good spiritual exercise to review one's day as you go to bed: thanks for helping me try and often succeed – but thanks even more for having already forgiven me for "little" sins and "bigger" ones, too – because of Jesus!

Which leads me to tell a kind of parable which we can see in our preparing for Christmas by putting up a Christmas tree. Part of that preparing is cleaning up the space – and maybe the whole room – where you will put the tree. Most likely you will do some dusting and sweeping and getting rid of old newspapers and magazines which may have piled up (as they usually do in most homes). So we prepare for the tree by getting rid of some "bad" things. Similarly, we spiritually prepare for Christmas (but also for every day) by getting rid of the bad we've done. Well, we can't completely "get rid of" "the bad" in our lives. It can be forgiven, but it will still hang around to mislead us – just like dust and dirt will never be completely gotten rid of from a room. However, part one of the preparing we do for Christmas is trying to get rid of the negative.

O.K. The place for the tree has been prepared, and the tree is in place. Then what? Decorations, of course! And each tree is decorated uniquely – according to the tastes and abilities of the family, usually of the mother. I remember from so long ago that some of us kids in our family used to kind of laugh about our Mom's "candy store tree" (as I think we called it), not because of a lot of candy on it, but because of all the glittering ornaments and lights. In Germany I experienced my relatives' tree with straw ornaments, actual lighted candles, and spun glass "angel hair". Each family beautifully decorates its tree uniquely.

We might say that faith in Jesus is the "Christmas tree" of our life. It (faith) springs to life by the work of the Holy Spirit working in us through the good news of Jesus, Who gave His life for us, which "news" comes to us both spoken and applied (through Baptism – and then kept alive also through Holy Communion). As a Christmas tree does not get into place by itself but by the work of the family members, so faith does not arise out of itself but by the work of God.

We have faith in place in us, right? What will be the

"decorations" on our faith "tree"? This is where our text instructs us. "You were once darkness, but now you are light in the Lord. Live as children of light" which is to live with "goodness, righteousness and truth" and with "what pleases the Lord". Which means: "Have nothing to do with the fruitless deeds of darkness" – that's the getting rid of the dirt preparation. And the positive "decorations"? "Be very careful, then, how you live...as wise, making the most of every opportunity...understand what the Lord's will is." The "decorations" for our "tree" of faith are to be the good things we do as we live daily, the things that please the Lord. It takes thinking and planning and positive effort. We are to hear God's Word and then learn to "understand" how it applies to us in our individual lives. What is the Lord's "will" for me? And His "will" is not merely His bare commands but His unique plan for my life. Our lives are all different with different opportunities in living His way. So He instructs us here: "making the most of every opportunity".

How does He want you to live with "goodness, righteousness and truth" this day, this week? Your life is unique! Your life as a "child of light" will be different from any other follower of Jesus. Similarities, of course – just like Christmas tree decorations have some shapes identical from one family's tree to another's, although arranged in a unique way. So our lives as His children have some identical characteristics: we keep trying to keep away from the sin He forbids and keep doing the good He commands. But this all happens uniquely, as we live out the plan He has for each of us.

One of my unique "tree decorations" is writing this weekly "Message", which you are not doing. You may be giving yourself in volunteering with a particular charity. Not everyone can be in your church's choir. You may be able to teach Sunday School or lead an at-home Bible study group. How you live in your family and at your job or as you shop is uniquely you as a "child of light". What are the unique ways you have opportunity to do for our Savior? These are the "decorations" on our "tree" of faith: lived actions which others can see we are doing. Others may take what we do for granted without much thought. But we know why we do these: to honor and thank Him!

For the One Whose coming we will soon be celebrating came to wake us up from the sleep of spiritual death. No matter whether we felt it or not, we all were "dead in trespasses and sins" (Ephesians 2:1). "But because of His great love for us, God, Who is rich in mercy, made us alive in Christ even when we were dead in transgressions – it is by grace you have been saved" (Ephesians 2:4-5). God the Holy Spirit worked through the good news message of Jesus as Savior to convince us, to make us spiritually alive, to have the "tree" of faith in Jesus.

So, we are to spiritually prepare, not just for a Christmas celebration, only to put all the decorations away afterward. No, we make these "decorations" of good deeds day by day, year by year, so that others "may see your good deeds and praise your Father in heaven" (Matthew 5:16), because your "light" shines into their "darkness" so that His good news message can become the good news of light and eternal life for them.

Which is not, therefore, only a December project, but is His "will", His plan, for us according to the opportunities He gives us, as we live day by day all year long.

December 8, 2013

Theme: **Advent – Message**

Related Reading: Luke 1:26-38

Text: Ephesians 3:1-13

ADVENT: THE MESSAGE WE HEAR

Along about now many of us might be beginning to feel somewhat overwhelmed: so much still to do and Christmas only a few days away! Are you feeling that way today? And even if you aren't this Christmas, sometimes that's how we feel in our lives: so much to do, so little time, so that our daily devotions or Bible reading gets pushed aside with a "don't have time for that today"! It happens, doesn't it!

Which is why God has commanded: O.K., My children, no excuses! Take the time to come to My Word! You need this break in your busy lives, a time to hear from Me in a comforting and refreshing way, so you'll be better able to handle the pressures and rush of your weekday living.

Not that every worship service is "comforting and refreshing". Sometimes the worship ritual seems boring (although is that because of how it is led or because of our inattentiveness?) – sometimes the preacher just lays down more law – sometimes the preacher forgets to make the good news of forgiveness clear and meaningful.

But God's purpose by having commanded weekly worship is first to comfort us: yes, you fell short again this week, but I gave My Son so that through forgiveness I pick you up again; and then secondly, to refresh us: remember always that not only do I call you to follow My way all week long, but also I am with you to help you face all the challenges of life in following Me. Which is not really "news" to us, since it's what we've heard week after week, but it is God's truth for us which will help us as we consciously try to think it through, as it is being proclaimed to us.

There isn't anything really "new" in this "Message", but it will be "true" – and, I pray, presented in a way that will be a little bit different so that you will "think it through". And the "little bit different" way is in Paul's talking about the mystery which he has been privileged to understand personally so he could share it with everyone else.

"Mystery"! Paul's Jewish readers would be tempted to think that it surely is a mystery how Gentiles, people who have been so steeped in superstition and idolatry and immorality and drunkenness (for this was the typical non-Jewish way of living then) – how could such people ever be allowed to become part of God's family and kingdom? Sure, God had told Abraham that "all peoples on earth will be blessed through you" (Genesis 12:3), specifically through Abraham's "seed", one specific descendant (Genesis 22:18). But surely that meant those evil people would have to become Jews like us in order to be blessed!

Such bias against Gentiles, non-Jews, had continued in the church for years; in fact, "Judaizers" is what those who believed this were called, although such who believed this

16

were not actually trusting in Jesus as Savior at all, as Paul clearly warned in the letter to the Galatians.

Actually, the pride of Jewish background Christians, since they still had their sinful natures, blinded them to the other part of this "mystery", the "mystery" of how even the Jewish people could be blessed eternally by God. For in their history they had been just as evil as the Gentiles! And in their self-righteous pride in themselves and in their Jewish ceremonies, they, too, were falling short of God's requirements and so were living in rebellion. This pride continued to be a temptation for Jewish Christians, those who did humbly admit they failed God and that their only hope was in Jesus – still they wondered, no, doubted that Gentiles could be accepted. Therefore, Paul and the other inspired writers had to keep telling them: Look in the mirror, folks! How is it possible that the holy God could ever accept unholy, sinful, rebellious you?!? Mystery!

Mystery solved, however, proclaims Paul – in our text and in all his inspired writings. God's solution was Jesus, God come to earth, Immanuel. Which is its own "mystery" in itself! For how could God become a human man at all? God Who is everywhere at once confined in a touchable body? God Who is almighty being a helpless baby – and a weak adult (weak compared to God, that is)? This mystery, of course, cannot be explained – God just did it: "conceived by the Holy Spirit, born of the Virgin Mary", impossible, but done!

The mystery of salvation – for Jews and Gentles – can be explained, however. This Jesus, Whose coming into human life we celebrate at Christmas, He was how God dealt with human sin. Being God come to earth, Jesus was big enough, one could say, so He could accept the burden of responsibility for all the people who have ever lived, responsibility for their obedience, responsibility for their punishment, since they – we – haven't obeyed.

First He obeyed – perfectly from the first breath of life to His last, never a sin, not once! Had to be, else how could He be punished for the sins of everyone else, if He had sins of His own which needed to be punished? And so Mary must have wondered: such a good baby – and Joseph must have wondered, as He grew up: such a good boy, never any trouble at all, fun-loving but helpful and obedient. At first, of course, they remembered: He is special – from God – angels told us – and others. But as the years went by, He was so ordinary – except never any trouble or into trouble – that by the time He was twelve, even they had forgotten Who He actually was: God with us on earth! Then in adulthood it was a bit odd that He didn't get married as other Jewish boys did, but He never did a single wrong thing, never!

Which had to be! Because He was obeying perfectly in the place of all of us who don't obey! All of us! In our place!

And then the punishment, as perhaps best expressed in Isaiah's prophecy: "We all, like sheep, have gone astray, each of us has turned to his own way, and the Lord has laid on Him the iniquity of us all" (Isaiah 53:6) – for punishment! Carried out on that cross – outside of Jerusalem – six hours of human time but an eternity in God's view, because there and then He endured the eternal punishment for sin! Which no one except Him could survive!

All of which would still be an unexplained mystery if all one could see were the historical facts: a human, born in poverty, unusually good life, yes, and a cruel death, even a tragic miscarriage of justice!

But there is that other fact of history: He did not stay dead! He rose to life again! So what do we make of that? Human thinking says: never happened, either because He never actually died, just appeared dead – oh, even though a spear into His side? – or His body was stolen and His disciples lied about it – or they were so emotionally wrought up that they hallucinated and only thought He had risen (these, you know, are the arguments unbelievers still use today).

Instead, God revealed to Paul and the other apostles: His resurrection means that what He did by obedience and by punishment has satisfied God's justice so that in this way He has paid for the gift of forgiveness of sins and eternal life for all sinners, for every single one.

That is the message we hear when God's good news is explained. But will we benefit? For it is not automatic for everyone: everyone could benefit, but human pride keeps most people from trusting this message as God's truth, and so they go their own way away from God.

But we have heard this message, and it has wiped out our pride and given us peace instead: I don't deserve it – every day I show that I don't – but God for Jesus' sake accepts me anyway. He frees me from my guilt, no matter what I have done. He also frees me from having to keep doing the sins I have done. And He helps me follow His way in the confidence that He will take care of me no matter what happens in life.

Which is why Paul concludes in our text that "through faith in Him we may approach God with freedom and confidence", freed from sin, confident of His care. That is the comfort and refreshment God wants us to have each week, as we take time to hear His message about Jesus so that then we can live the week for Him.

December 15, 2013

Theme: **Advent – Joy**

Related Reading: Matthew 1:18-25

Text: 1 John 3:1-13

ADVENT: THE JOY WE HAVE

Joy, the joy John had according to our text! But how can we have that joy, because John had distinct advantages over us. After all, as he wrote, he had seen and touched and heard Jesus in the flesh. But all we have are words, words about Jesus.

However, before we get even a little bit envious of John or the other disciples, let's recognize that while they were hearing, seeing, and touching Jesus, they didn't realize Who He actually was. Yes, they believed He was the Promised One of God, the Messiah, but they didn't realize He was God on earth! And why didn't they? Because He was so human with them, just like one of them, although never doing anything wrong that they ever noticed. But He was just their brother and cousin and friend, because they heard Him snore and saw Him spit and laughed at His jokes! Oh, did you never think Jesus told jokes? Why not? He was human, wasn't He? And He not only was tempted in every way as we are, but He participated in life as we do – except for not sinning. So, no wonder that even after He had risen from the dead, they still expected Him to set up a human kingdom on earth, the "kingdom of heaven", for didn't they ask on Ascension Day: "Lord, are You at this time going to restore the kingdom to Israel?" (Acts 1:6). The plain truth is that while they were with Him personally, they did not realize that He was "the Word of Life"!

In fact, while Jesus was alive on earth in His human life, maybe only a dozen or so people recognized Him as the Savior come to earth: Mary and Joseph, because they had been told by angels; maybe half a dozen shepherds, again because they had been told by the angel and the angelic choir; Simeon and Anna in the temple, also because God had revealed it to Simeon; and then the Wise Men, who also worshiped Him, but only because Herod's priests had told them from God's Word, the prophet Micah, that the Promised One would be born in Bethlehem. These folks worshiped Jesus as Savior in those first months of His life. But later on not even Mary and Joseph remembered this always – because He lived such a human life.

So, the fact is we are no worse off than the disciples regarding our recognizing Jesus as the Savior: they needed God's Word on Pentecost to learn this fact; that's how we learn also: He is the Savior, because God's Word says so. And so we also can have the same joy which they had – on the basis of God's Word.

Which is why, most probably, John in our text wrote this somewhat strange concluding sentence: "We write this to you to make our joy complete." For he wrote so that more sinners, you and me included, would through his inspired writing come into and have the joy of knowing Jesus as the Word of life, giving us eternal life as well as joy in this life.

For, as I just personally experienced this past week, what a joy to help two unbelievers come to see – and, I trust, to believe – that "the wages of sin is death, but the gift of God is eternal life in Christ Jesus our Lord" (Romans 6:23). To have that joy for one's self and then to have others also come into that joy, well, that's what John meant: "to make our joy complete".

But why did John even write in this way to assure his readers that Jesus really had existed as a Person, as God on earth? We could ask the same question of Paul: why did he write 1 Corinthians 15, the great "Resurrection" chapter, with his listing of all who had seen Jesus resurrected, even 500 at once? Because people then had their doubts, had their times of: that can't be! God on earth, Immanuel, in one little baby? Can't be! Impossible! A person definitely dead but then raised to life again? Can't be! Impossible! So they were inspired to write in this very human way: we and others actually saw Him, actually lived with Him, He truly is the Savior, our Savior! As people listened, the Holy Spirit could work to bring them to faith in this "Word of Life" and to keep them in faith.

Which is what He does in us. We hear – we think – we realize by the Holy Spirit's power: yes, God truly did come to earth as a Baby becoming a Man to be the Savior. For that is really what John and Paul and all the Bible writers were aiming at: not merely the "what", but the "what for", the purpose. Just to think about a helpless baby is meaningless in itself – helpless babies are born every day. Just to think about a man dying an unjust, agonizing death is meaningless – two others died the same way, although for just cause, that same day. But the "why" of it, the meaning, the purpose: by His life and death He is the Savior, He is the Word of Life! That is what gives sinners joy, that is what gives us joy: the Word of Life!

For we live in a world of death, not just physical death which we all will experience (unless Judgment Day comes first), but especially spiritual death. All we have to do is look around us and hear the news: people enduring meaningless lives with escapism into drugs and sex and excitement their only relief from meaninglessness. Yet even these are meaningless, as Solomon wrote in Ecclesiastes. True, there are the pleasures of family and friends, of helping others. But no matter how much we enjoy these, they, too, end up meaningless, for death takes them all away.

But we have real joy, when we trust in Jesus as the only Savior. We know that there is more to life than just living here on earth; Jesus has lived and died and risen to give us eternal life. And we know His promises to watch over us and work out for good whatever happens in this life, if we are trusting in Him. That's the underlying joy we have, even when our living day by day seems pointless (for some times it does for all of us), even when life suddenly turns disastrous or brings about big changes in our plans and expectations (such as a trip on a corner and suddenly a broken hip, as I just experienced) – no matter – we are in His care, because He gave Himself for us. Joy!

John had joy! So do we! For the same reason! Because Jesus came and lived, but even more, suffered and died for us sinners to give us the gift of eternal life.

December 22, 2013

Theme: **Christmas**

Related Reading: Luke 2:1-20

Text: Luke 2:8-14

PEACE, GOOD WILL – TOWARD ALL

It was a quiet night, flickering fire warming a couple of shepherds, awake because it was their turn to guard the sheep; occasionally they heard the low bleating of their sheep, but quiet.

Then SUDDENLY! Startled by a light like they had never seen before! And it shone just on them! They were terrified! Who wouldn't be?

Then a voice! Telling about: good news – a baby has been born – to bring joy for all people, because this Baby is the Savior! Christ! The Lord! And then a sound like rolling thunder: angel voices, a multitude! And what was that they said? Glory! Peace! Good Will! Toward All!

Then, just as suddenly, it was over – done – ended!

Or was it? Not at all – in fact, it had just begun! Wasn't ended for the shepherds – they went to see – and came away singing! And it had just begun for the One born that night, because the cave-barn led to a hill – the manger led to a cross. His life was not intended merely to bring joy to one family, but to make joy possible for all people, because He was the Savior for all sinners, all people. That's not only what one angel said – that's what all the angels proclaimed, because the peace they sang of was not a peace between nations or even peace between individuals. They meant peace with God through the forgiveness of sins. And the good will they announced means not a Christmas spirit of kindness and sharing, but God's good will for salvation, the same good will of God as described by John (3:16): "God loved the world so that He gave His one and only Son that whoever believes in Him shall not perish but have eternal life".

Oh, how we need that peace, that good will, that forgiveness, that salvation! For the darkness of that first Christmas night and that flock of sheep needing a shepherd guard are perfect symbols for the need of salvation that we all have. For we are like sheep, sheep who wander around almost blindly, seeing little further than the grass in front of their noses. And we like sheep do what we think is best and right, but we are limited by spiritual short-sightedness and are misled by the darkness of the sinful nature still in each of us.

True, often we really try to do our best; yet we still never obey God perfectly – and sometimes we just give in to willingly follow our evil desires or the spiritual darkness of the world around us. So, we are lost – on our own, without hope before God – on our own – because of our sinfulness. It's not just evil people who are hope-less; we also are hope-less before Him – on our own. We ordinary, well-meaning but sinful people, ornery people even, we need someone to save us.

27

And that Someone came – that's what Christmas is all about: the One Who came to earn and bring peace to us, the One Who came to a manger in Bethlehem for a cross near Jerusalem. He came because of God's good will, God's love which does not want any to perish forever, God's love which wants us to be with Him in glory, not apart from Him in damnation.

So God planned His coming already from eternity – and not just His coming, but especially His work of paying for our sins. As the prophet Isaiah (53:6) had said more than 700 years beforehand: "We all like sheep have gone astray, each of us has turned to his own way; and the Lord has laid on Him the iniquity (the guilt) of us all." That's why He came – because of our guilt – to pay for our sins: not there in the manger – that was only the beginning, not even as He lived – that was essential yet only preliminary, but there on His cross – that's where He gave Himself for us, for all.

Yes, God's intention and plan is to benefit all, you and me, but also everyone else. God sends His peace, good will – toward all! Jesus came for all so that whoever does believe in Him (that is, depends on Him) will receive eternal life.

Which means that if we are to benefit from Jesus' coming, if we are to enjoy God's peace and good will, then we must depend not on anything we do for God, because we cannot do enough, we cannot be good enough; but we must depend only on Jesus and what He has done for us – from His manger to His cross – paying for us sinners by His perfect life and by His suffering and death. Then, because of Him we have peace with God because our sins are forgiven; and because of Him we have assurance of God's good will not only here in time, but throughout all eternity.

That's not all, however! Because, remember, God's peace and good will is "toward all"! This good news is too good to hoard – this good news is to share, to tell others personally, even as the shepherds did, by telling family and friends: I have some good news that I want you to know – Jesus truly is God's good news for us sinners – come with me to hear how He gives us peace with God and how God's good will can work in our lives, even in our day to day living; Jesus is my joy – I want you to have joy in Him, too!

This is how we help the angel's message of the first Christmas night become reality in our day: Peace – Good Will – Toward All!

December 24, 2007

Theme: **New Year**

Related Reading: Luke 13:6-9

Text: Philippians 3:12-14

QUO VADIS IN THIS NEW YEAR?

The Latin question "Quo vadis", where are you going, is according to a Christian tradition the question Peter asked Jesus in a vision he saw of Jesus walking toward Rome from which Peter was fleeing because of threatening persecution. According to this story – and it is only a story – Jesus answered: I'm going to Rome – to be crucified. Which soundly struck Peter's conscience: my Savior is willing to die again, because I'm afraid to die for Him? So Peter turned back to Rome and eventually was crucified in Nero's persecution of the early church. So did Peter "glorify God" by the death he died (which Jesus had predicted in John 21:29).

None of us will see such a vision of Jesus nor will we suffer crucifixion persecution as Peter did. However, as we look ahead at the beginning of a new year, the question: "Quo vadis, where are you going?" is a good one to consider. Where are we going in this new year of 2014? We can't say for sure, of course, since none of us knows what the future holds. However, what we can foresee – or suspect we see – can make us fearful for our personal safety, although not as much as Peter was for his.

First, quo vadis, America? Yes, where is our country

going health-wise, given what we've experienced so far of Obamacare? Quo vadis, America? Where is our country going politically as so many extremists seem to be becoming more and more hate-filled and even obscene in their opposition to the "other side" (and, if you think that conservatives are the guilty ones in this, you should read the "letters to the editor" page in our local newspaper from professed "liberals")? And, quo vadis, America, economically as governmental debt continues to balloon, well above $17 trillion now – and growing – with the job market still mostly in reverse? Doesn't look too good where America is heading. And we can't do much about it (except to be sure that in political discussion we will be honest, reasonable, and courteous). Doesn't look too good, but even so, most likely none of these negative prospects will really hurt us personally all that much.

However, there is another "Quo vadis, America?" which does pose real danger, spiritual danger. Quo vadis, America, morally and spiritually? For unbelievers and those promoting immorality are becoming more and more vocal in condemning Christian values and principles in our country. Especially homosexual pressure groups rise up to condemn any expression of opposition to their perversions – for that is what that lifestyle is: perversion – God's Word says so, not me. As also God's Word says that heterosexual immorality is perversion and not to be approved of by His people. But no matter that we Americans are supposed to have the constitutional right to practice – and promote – our religious convictions without governmental interference and restrictions, that right is not respected by those who reject any opposition especially to their sexual activities. Quo vadis, America, spiritually and morally? Increasingly the direction our country seems to be going will result in outright persecution, probably in the form of extreme fines (as is the case already under ObamaCare) or even jail time (as is happening in Canada already) for us who stand firm in our Christian convictions.

All of which leads us to the kind of "Quo vadis" implications of our text: Quo vadis, where are you going, Christian, spiritually in this new year? Will we remain faithful in following our Savior according also to His guiding in life principles or will we give in and go along with where our country will go? This has always been a temptation for us (to go along with the ways of unbelievers, that is), but it will become even more of a temptation, if it begins to cost us money in the form of fines or even threatened jail time. So, quo vadis – where are you going to be going as a child of God, a follower of Jesus, a truster in Jesus in this new year?

We, of course, as I mentioned earlier, we don't know all that may happen to us, which may change our plans and dreams for this year. My recent little stumble resulting in the broken hip will drastically change my life-style, probably for at least six months, if not permanently – who would think a single stumble could cause that? Nor does any of us know what the flu might do to us – or some other virulent illness which can strike so unexpectedly. Quo vadis, where are we going physically this year? We don't know – only the Lord does. He promises to work for good to us, even if hurt happens – including the hurt of persecution; but only He knows now whether there will be extra hurt or real persecution and what the good might be in His plan for us in this coming year.

Our text, however, asks us that "quo vadis, where are you going?" question in a different way. Paul uses himself as example. He had truly been serving the Lord well, following His guidance carefully. And yet he had to admit: not as well as I should have. So he confesses: "Not that I have already obtained or already been made perfect." He was looking toward serving the Lord perfectly in eternity, but he was not there yet. We might think he was so great a servant of the Lord, especially in comparison to ourselves, but he says: Doesn't matter what I have done, there is better ahead of me: "Forgetting what is behind and striving toward what is ahead, I press on toward the goal to win the prize for which God has called me heavenward in Christ Jesus" – yes, I've done a bunch, but there is more to do, much more. And there is no resting on my past accomplishments; that I have to leave behind and just look ahead to what He wants me to do.

Yes, Paul, you better not "rest on your laurels" – and you had best "forget what is behind", because, as you yourself have admitted, you still have remained a sinner, even "the chief of sinners", as far as you could tell, as you wrote to Timothy (I,1,9). So what is Paul's hope, his confidence before God? At first glance it almost sounds as though he has to earn it, since he writes in our text how he must "press on ... to win the prize for which God has called me". Yet he can't mean that he contributes even an ounce toward deserving or earning that prize of eternal life. For he so often and so clearly says it is only through Jesus and what Jesus has done. Even here he says: "God has called me heavenward in Christ Jesus"! No, Paul trusts not at all in what he did or does – but only is thankful for how the Lord has used him and accomplished much through his efforts. All he does is thanks for what God has done for him in Christ Jesus.

Which means also for us that we can be thankful when we can honestly see some ways the Lord has used us in His work. Although we never do good enough, we are thankful for what good we did do for the Lord in this past year – being thankful keeps it in the right perspective.

But then Paul is teaching also us: Quo vadis? Where will you be going now in this new year? What now can you do in serving Him? Forget how you did serve – look forward to what you now can do!

Which does not necessarily mean that we will do more in the quantity of what we will do, such as, if you gave $100 for the Lord's work in 2013, then you will need to give at least that much and even more! Or, if you gave of your time each week to serve in some particular program of helping others, that you will have to give more time. Our resources aren't the same – our energy isn't either – nor are our opportunities, meaning, the Lord may guide you toward something new (a new neighbor to help, for example) so that you may not have as much time for things you did this past year. Life changes – our ways of serving the Lord do also. But we are to keep serving in what seems to be the most effective way we can. That is doing as Paul writes; "Forgetting what is behind and straining toward what is ahead, I press on toward the goal to win" – well, let's make that easier to keep clear, so "to receive the prize for which God has called me heavenward in Christ Jesus."

For do you hear how Paul always does keep that clear? We never deserve the prize of eternal life, for it is God's gift to us. He gives it since He paid for it through the work of Jesus – we are "called heavenward in Christ Jesus". What we do is strictly our response of thanks for His gift – strictly! Completely!

Yet it requires our effort! Paul says we will have to "strain" as he did. Why? Partly because of all those "quo vadis, America?" situations which will affect us and which will make life tougher for us, perhaps physically and economically, but especially spiritually. We will continually in this new year need to be looking to Him for the assurance of forgiveness and for the guidance we need to keep choosing what is good and right in spite of being tempted otherwise.

Quo vadis, my friends, in this new year? Because of His call of grace, because of how He has worked in Christ Jesus to make us His, because of His continuing to be with us to help us endure what will come and to see the good He is working for us and through us, yes, because of what He has done, we enter this new year with the prayer: *Help me, Lord, to be faithful to You in this new year, because You will love and forgive and help me each day that does come. Amen.*

January 1, 2014

Theme: **Epiphany – For the Whole World**
Related Reading: Matthew 2:1-12
Text: Luke 4:42-44

WE ALSO ARE SENT

As we begin a new year, it is totally unknown to us – we cannot know what it will bring. Although we pray for a "happy" – a good – "new year", ominous things could happen, we may have to suffer much. Yet, if that should come, we have God's promise to take care of us through heartache as well as happiness, all the way into eternity. That's why Jesus came! That's why He was sent!

Nothing unknown to Him as He came, however. He knew the cross awaited Him so that all people from every nation could be rescued from their sins. That's the meaning of Epiphany, the celebration of the coming of the so-called "Wise Men" to Bethlehem to the recently-born Jesus – Who, by the way, was more than 40 days old by the time they finally saw Him, if you carefully read Luke 2 as well as Matthew 2. The eternal plan of the Triune God would be carried out. He would do it! And we – by faith in Him – would benefit.

The Lord, however, does not promise to take care of us whatever happens so we can just live our lives as we please for ourselves. He takes care of us so He can use us in His ongoing plan for the people of this world. He sent Jesus, of course, to do the biggest job, the job only God come to earth,

God with us, Immanuel, could do. Only He could live life perfectly – only He could give His life sacrificially in payment for the sins of everyone.

But God's plan is not yet completed. And just as God had to use a human tool (Jesus, fully human as well as fully God) for that biggest part of His plan, so He needs us as His human tools to complete His plan. "To complete His plan"? Yes! For what good does Jesus' obeying and paying do for sinners who never hear that message, that good news? He has to use human tongues and human writing to get this message to sinners.

Well, of course! That means those humans called pastors and missionaries, doesn't it? They are sent by God to speak to others, aren't they? Sorry, folks! Not only them! We also are sent! For we have opportunities to speak to others which pastors and missionaries will never have! And the Lord needs to use us as His tools. That's how we also are sent into this new year: to reach others with the good news of Jesus as Savior.

However, we don't always have speaking opportunities with other sinners. Well, of course we do – we talk to other people every day. Still, it doesn't work to just spout off every time you see someone about Jesus dying on the cross – people, sinful people, so easily can close their ears and their minds as though you are just a kook! Think what many people have said about Tim Tebow for his continual talk about thanking Jesus for his athletic success! You and I need to earn the willingness of others to listen. And for that job we also are sent. In other words, there are things that need to be done before we have the right to speak the things that need to be said. And often these are very ordinary things.

In our text Jesus says: "I must preach the good news of the kingdom of God to other towns also, because this is why I was sent." But You were sent to die on the cross as Savior, weren't You, Jesus? To be sure! Still, there were steps which had to be taken, tasks which had to be done, in order to get to that cross – and in order to get people prepared to listen to the meaning of that cross! How do you think it was possible for 3000 people to come to faith in Jesus all on Pentecost Sunday 50 days after Jesus' resurrection – with thousands more also coming to faith in the following weeks (Acts 2:41,3:4)? Jesus' preaching had begun to open their hearts and minds so that when the final explanation was revealed on and after Pentecost, so many people so quickly came to faith, responding: Ah! That's why He came! That's what it all means! That's what He did! For me! The turning from unbelief to faith in Jesus does not happen like lightening out of a clear sky! There has to be preparation! Things have to happen so people will listen and think and finally be convinced: yes, Jesus did this because of sin – because of my sin – Jesus did this for me!

That's how you and I came to faith or have remained in faith. True, Baptism as a baby started many of us on the path of faith. But then we had to not only keep hearing the good news, but also keep seeing it in action in the lives of those who confessed that faith. How many baptized children have lost their infant faith either because no one kept telling them the meaning of Jesus or because someone so clearly contradicted the faith they claimed by the unbelieving life they lived so that the child reacted: What a farce! Not for me! This happens, folks! Frankly, it happened to me – until by God's grace I was brought back to faith. How gracious He was – and is – to me.

So, do you see from this reality part of how we also are sent by God into this new year? He needs us to do those preliminary things first of all so that we can then share the good news of Jesus, the preliminary things of building relationships with people until we are able to talk with them about faith.

The first step in that is to consider to whom the Lord has sent you for such a relationship. For the Lord puts us into where we live our lives and puts us into contact with people whom He wants to reach with the Gospel message. Who is it especially for you? A neighbor? Someone at work? A relative whom you know does not follow Jesus in faith? For myself there are two neighbors especially whom I think the Lord wants me to reach out to. Frankly, I've known them now for over a year – and I've been concerned for them – and I've tried to be friendly with them. But in preparing this message I've realized more clearly that I need to do more with God's aim in mind. I pray that in this year I will do that – and perhaps find a way to speak seriously with them about faith in Jesus. I don't know how it will work out, but the Lord has put these two individuals into my life for this purpose I am convinced. Whom has He put into your life? Whom is He sending you to?

Should we build relationships with others with that ulterior motive of perhaps being able to speak to them of Jesus? Not if that's the only reason we try to help and become friends: so that we feel justified in dropping them if they never respond! We are to do good, because this is helping others in their needs. We are to be friendly, because this is good to do. But it's not wrong to have a plan for more than mere human activities. In fact, how else will we be able to share God's good news with someone unless we know that person as a friend? Why did Jesus not only go out to preach to "other towns" but even go to banquets with prostitutes and tax collectors, the "scum of society", "sinners", as people then called them (example, Matthew 9:10-12), other than to have them get to know Him so they would listen to Him? Remember: God has to use us humans as His tools – and we have to take the preliminary steps, if we are to accomplish the mission God has sent us to carry out.

That being said, we also must admit that it's kind of scary – for me, too. So we pray for opportunity, for courage, for wisdom, for help, because we truly do want our friends and acquaintances to have the peace with God which we have because of Jesus, don't we?

And as we ask the Lord's guidance and help, He will use

us in His grand plan to bring sinners into His eternal family through faith in Jesus. He will – because we are the only tools He now has available.

Lord, help us so to serve You in this coming year, since You came and gave Yourself for us and also for these other people whom I know need You. Amen.

January 8, 2012

Theme: **Life Sunday**

Related Reading: Psalm 139:1-16

Text: Luke 1:39-45

MY BABY KICKED ME!

"Come, honey! Feel! Our baby just kicked me!" Said the first-time mother-to-be to the first time father-to-be. Even though, as an experienced mother explained to me, the baby probably only moved, not kicked, still, what a thrill! Maybe not enough to make up for all those days of morning sickness, yet, quite a thrill! And proof for what every natural mother knows: this is a baby growing within me, not just a group of cells, growing like a cancer, as those who have been satanically perverted try to believe so they can excuse abortion.

But try as those murderers might – for, if it is a baby, a human life, then to get rid of it is to murder that child – and try as they might to excuse this evil, every mother-to-be knows: my baby! If not so, then why is there so much guilt after an abortion? If not so, then why do thoughts come: what would he or she be like today – as a character in a movie I recently viewed said just seemingly "out of the blue" to a newly-met friend: I thought it had to be, but... was her anguished statement – and this was not a Christian or a pro-life movie, just a realistic movie about two lonely people. Yes, every pregnant woman knows, unless she has become hardened and ruthless: my baby!

This abortion business – and that's what it is primarily, a business to make money – is so evil. So it tries to make up excuses: just a bunch of cells of a female body – also, think of all the stem cell good that can be done with those embryonic stem cells. Say, maybe there's something to that! Did you hear that recently a man received a trachea implant, which had been grown from stem cells? Oops! Not embryonic stem cells obtained by killing a yet-to-be-born baby or even obtained from an umbilical cord, but from what are called "adult stem cells", taken from that man's own body! The fact is: embryonic stem cell research has not yet produced even one health benefit, while adult stem cell research has produced healing results for many, many people. Another abortionist excuse shown to be a lie!

In being so blunt about babies not yet born and how abortion murders them, I do not want to increase the guilt which any of you might already feel if you have had an abortion or urged someone to have an abortion – you have more than enough guilt already – which we will deal with in just a few minutes. However, if you feel no guilt, then you should, for you are in deep spiritual trouble. In fact, see what God's Word says about a murderer in 1 John 3:15. And I am not trying to make abortion be the worst sin possible. The 1 John passage clearly teaches that hatred is just as serious as murder. And elsewhere in Scripture, specifically 1 Corinthians 6 and Galatians 5 and Colossians 3, other evils are just as much unbelief as murder or hatred (the Colossians verses even specify "greed" as unbelieving evil, for it is idolatry) – so easily any of us can fall away into the unbelief of actions, which absolutely contradict mere words about believing!

We all are guilty in our own ways, whether of faith-destroying evil or of perfection-destroying daily sinning! Inexcusably guilty – so that we all must say, as St. Paul almost despairingly said: "What a wretched man I am! Who will rescue me from this body of death?" (Romans 7:24) Impossible! Hopeless! That is how we should feel – when examining ourselves! Me, too, as I remember certain deeds in my life, also some acts of inexcusable cruelty, not of deeds, but of words. No matter your evil or mine, how can the burden of guilt be lifted from us? It truly seems impossible, especially when it is something that strikes us so deeply emotionally, such as abortion can – or whatever evil lurks in your memory!

Which is how the birth of a baby physically can teach us spiritually. For that baby began by God's guidance from just two tiny cells, too small for the naked eye to see. But God caused them to unite according to His plan – and, yes, even conception caused by rape or incest is according to His plan – not that God caused the evil deeds – evil is human responsibility completely; but God still works and has a plan for that conceived baby. That conception – and that continuing growth into the baby which finally moves or actually kicks or, as Elizabeth said in our text: "the baby in my womb leaped for joy" when the sound of Mary's greeting reached her ears – that growth into a moving baby with finally birth is a physical miracle! Just happened by evolutionary chance? How ridiculous to believe such a lie! Each baby is a miracle of God! By His creative power! Impossible! But He does it!

Which is how we are to think and believe and know about the spiritual miracle God worked out through "the mother of my Lord", as Elizabeth said. The miracle of God in His love for us sinners, for us, no matter what we have been guilty of: abortion, murder, hate, cruelty, immorality, drunkenness, greed, no matter what, the miracle God worked so we who are inexcusably guilty might have comfort and peace, that miracle is Jesus, come to earth through conception by the Holy Spirit. And when did Jesus bring humanity into His divinity? Only when He was born, finally delivered out of Mary's womb? Nonsense! From the first moment of conception Jesus became the God/man, Immanuel, God with us sinners here in human life. A baby begins at conception, not only after there is a recognizable body which moves or kicks or leaps – a baby, a living human being, begins when God causes those two cells to unite.

Jesus' conception, of course, did not use two human cells, but only one, Mary's ovum, fertilized by the power of the Holy Spirit – a miracle in itself! And then He grew in the womb and after nine months outside the womb and finally became that man, rather, that Immanuel, that God/man, on the cross where God's miracle of forgiveness was completed: all the sins of everyone – and that means the evils, too, the abortions and the murders and the hatreds and everything –

all suffered for – all paid for – all removed from our spiritual history in God's sight so we guilty people can have peace, peace about what we are guilty of, whatever it is, peace, as we depend on that spiritual miracle of Jesus and what He did as He lived, as He suffered, as He died.

Not that our guilt feelings never again attack us – the devil uses them to tell us: how terrible you are – no hope for you – bad, bad, bad! But we are not defenseless! As that great hymn by Martin Luther says: "He's (Jesus is) by our side upon the plain...one little word can fell him (the devil with his attacks)" – and that word, that little impossible but true word is: forgiven!

And so, when the crashing surf of guilt threatens us again, whatever guilt it is, that little word will be our weapon, our defense, our peace – as we repeat it to ourselves, as often as we need to, until the ocean of guilt ebbs away: forgiven! God's impossible, but actual, spiritual miracle: forgiven!

May we each use that good news word so we can leave guilt in order to live at peace with our God for Whom we now are living.

January 22, 2012

47

Theme: **Transfiguration**

Related Reading: Matthew 17:1-8

Text: Galatians 1:1-10

ABSOLUTELY NO COMPROMISE!

"Intolerant!   That's what you Christians are!   See what your Paul says right here: Anyone who does not believe exactly as he believes will be 'eternally condemned'!   How awful to be so arrogant!"   So would say modern unbelieving intellectuals – while other unbelievers merely dismiss what the Bible says as just so much nonsense.

Of course the "intolerant" accusers don't listen to exactly what Paul was inspired to write, because what he clearly says is that even if he should "change his tune" for any reason to preach to them a "different gospel", even he should be "eternally condemned".   By this he is emphasizing that there is only one "gospel", only one message of good news from God to sinners, the good news he had just mentioned: "Jesus Christ, Who gave Himself for our sins to rescue us from the present evil age", that is, from this life controlled by sin.   That "rescue" by Jesus is the "good news", the only "news" from God that is "good".

Which is why Paul is in effect saying there can be absolutely no compromise with any other message which anyone might claim to be from God – this message that Jesus is the "Rescuer" (which is what "Savior" actually means), this is the only way for any one to be rescued from their life of sin to enjoy the glory of God now and forever. Absolutely no compromise about it! None! If that is being "intolerant", so be it! We have to be uncompromising about the good news, for there is no other way!

Which is why unbelievers object to the Christian faith – and why also our sinful nature doesn't want to keep believing it, but is easily tempted to believe "a different gospel". What? You and I don't inwardly want to believe the real gospel? Of course I want to and do believe it, don't you? Still, when we think about all those other people, nice people, good people, you mean they are all to be "eternally condemned"? Doesn't seem fair – especially if they never had a chance to hear about Jesus, and especially if they are sincere in what they do believe – still they are "eternally condemned"? Surely there must be some other way for them to be rescued! Have you ever had thoughts like that? I have.

Which is our sinful nature talking, because deep down inside of us we still have that pat-yourself-on-the-back feeling of: I'm really not that bad a person, so God will accept me! Which is why the voice from heaven on the Transfiguration Mountain told the disciples (Matthew 17:1-8): "This is My Son Whom I love, with Him I am well-pleased. Listen to Him!" Don't listen to your proud ideas or to anyone else's human ideas no matter how reasonable they sound! Listen! To Him!

Which is why our God commands us to come to His

Word, especially His good news message of Jesus, our Rescuer, every week! We have to keep hearing it so the Holy Spirit can keep us believing it, depending on it, instead of giving in to our own pride and the pride of those who proclaim a "different gospel", a gospel which always includes the idea: it's up to you to do your part at least! No! Listen to Him, to Jesus! So you trust Him as your Rescuer, your Savior! Absolutely no compromise allowed!

This message won't make you popular with most people, however, as Paul writes in this text: "Am I trying to win the approval of men or of God?" and as he had warned the Thessalonians (I,3:3): "In fact, when we were with you, we kept telling you that we would be persecuted". That's the inescapable result when absolutely no compromise is allowed regarding God's good news of Jesus being the only Rescuer! Proud sinners don't like it and fight it! Even our sinful nature fights it inside of us – if we listen to our thoughts instead of to Jesus' Word.

However, we do have to be careful in this "no compromise" conviction. In human pride again we are tempted to apply this to whatever we say or think about the other beliefs of God's Word. Churches throughout the ages have fought over doctrine with the attitude that "if you don't agree in every detail of doctrine as I say it, then you aren't really a Christian at all!" But Paul specifies "the gospel of Christ". Which does include more than only John 3:16: "God so loved the world that He gave His one and only Son so that whoever believes in Him shall not perish but have eternal life". For there are other necessary teachings with that, such as: Jesus was God come to earth – through a virgin birth so He would be both God and man – that Jesus did rise from the dead – that God is the Triune God. This is why we have the Apostles' and Nicene Creeds: to summarize the teachings which are essential to the "good news" of Jesus. If a person denies any of these teachings, that person has rejected the good news of Jesus entirely., And again: there is absolutely no compromise about these essential teachings.

But there are other details of teachings which do not destroy the one good news message, such as, various teachings regarding both the end of this world and even the beginning of it. The end of this world and exactly what will happen then can be explained in different ways. It really should be clear if one looks at all of God's Word – but if one overemphasizes a few passages, one can come up with different teachings, which would not conflict with the essential message of Jesus, Who is the only way to get to the blessings at the end of this world. Christians should agree, but not all do, yet do not automatically compromise faith in Jesus alone.

Also regarding how this earth and life on it got here! Although it is actually irrational to believe that everything got here just by accident – especially when we think, for example, of how two different cells combined and then grew into a living person – by accident? Come on! Be reasonable! Yet some who do trust in Jesus as Rescuer also believe in evolution, that God used evolution to create everything. It is a contradiction to the clear teaching of what Jesus says through His Word, for the only way we can now "listen to Him" is through His inspired Word, the Bible. But some Christians swallow that contradiction without realizing its danger. For the belief of evolution is based on the belief that there is no "god" at all so that we are merely very temporary accidents of consciousness soon to be gone – forever – so, you better get whatever you can out of this brief time of existence. That atheistic and hopeless and materialistic belief of evolution can very easily kill faith in Jesus; but some Christians succeed – at least for a while – in believing those two contradictory things: Christian faith says – God exists and created us and wants us to live with Him forever; evolution belief says – no "god" – nothing! Such evolution belief will most likely eventually overwhelm faith in Jesus, because it appeals to human pride and our I-can-do-whatever-I-want attitude. That's why God tells us in our text: Don't listen to human ideas! Listen! To Him!

We should never compromise anything which Jesus, God come to earth, says in His Word, but especially no compromise at all about the essential good news message: No other way for sinners! Jesus is the only Rescuer!

Yet we are to be tolerant – not approving, but tolerant – of others in their wrong beliefs and their wrong deeds. It's the only way we can get to know them so that we can have the opportunity to share this good news with them, because Jesus came for them also. They will listen, however, only as they see the good Jesus enables us to do also for them.

And so God tells us to listen to Jesus daily by reading His Word and especially to hear His Word each week in public worship, for that's the only way we will keep on believing it and living it and sharing it.

March 10, 2011

Theme: **Palm Sunday**

Related Reading: Matthew 21:1-11

Text: Zechariah 9:9-10

HE CAME AND COMES FOR PEACE

Palm Sunday! What excitement! Hosanna! However! How much did those pilgrims, singing praise to God because of Jesus – "the prophet" they called Him (Matthew 21:11), understand? Very little! Even the disciples didn't understand on that day, for John writes: "At first His disciples did not understand all this. Only after Jesus was glorified did they realize these things had been written about Him" (12:16).

We look at the prophecy of our text and also see how Matthew quoted half of it (21:4-5), and it seems so clear. But the fact is that although some of the prophecies about the coming Messiah were very clear – remember how "the chief priests and teachers of the Law" knew that the Christ was to be born "in Bethlehem in Judea...for this is what the prophet has written" (Matthew 2:4-6), most of the prophecies were much more easily understood in hindsight rather than foresight – especially because so many of the prophecies seemed to be predicting military victory for Israel, a kingdom of earthly power. We have to sympathize with the Israelites before Jesus fulfilled the prophecies – it was tough for them to understand.

But we now can see what God meant! We can see why

Matthew quoted our text, at least the first part of it. How obvious! "See, your king comes to you...riding on a donkey, on a colt, the foal of a donkey" – how could the disciples, who knew the Hebrew Bible so well, as all the Israelite men did, how could they not have had even an inkling of a memory, as they used that little donkey colt for Jesus to ride on, at least one of them thinking: this sounds like what the prophet Zechariah wrote – could it be? But not one of them did – they were too caught up in the excitement perhaps. They didn't – but we do – because the Holy Spirit has explained it to us through the words of the New Testament.

And we understand not only the words about joyful shouting and Jesus riding on that little donkey, but we see clearly Zechariah's prophecy about why He came: to "proclaim peace", peace not just for the Israelites, but for "all nations...from sea to sea and from the River (meaning the Euphrates, which had special meaning for the Old Testament Israelites, for they had been carried off across it as captives) to the ends of the earth." And we know that He came and was even on Palm Sunday carrying out the process of establishing that peace, which already the angel had announced to the Bethlehem shepherds at His birth: "peace on earth".

Peace! How we long for peace! Peace in the world – peace in communities – peace in families (perhaps even in your own) – peace! End of fighting – end of killing – end of arguing – peace! How we long for peace!

Even while we recognize that such human peace will never be achieved in this world, not ever, let alone in our personal experience. It can't happen – because of sinful human nature. Pride and lust and revenge and greed will never be eradicated in this world, and these sinful desires will always cause conflict, whether family argument or nations at war. No peace possible, if absence of conflict is the definition of peace.

Still, the prophecy is: "He will proclaim peace to the nations". And the prophecy continues: "His rule will extend...to the ends of the earth". This king, Jesus, will rule a kingdom which is not defined by geographical boundaries, but by His rule in people within all geographical boundaries. For as Jesus said to Pilate: "My kingdom is not of this world" (John 18:36), but instead "the kingdom of God is within you" (Luke 17:21). The peace He proclaims is peace with God instead of war against God. This peace is what He was working at as He entered Jerusalem that day to the cheering of pilgrims. But He knew that parade would in five days turn into a cross-led trudge – to a low hill just outside of Jerusalem – the hill where His peace-making would be completed.

For that is what He was all about: to make peace between God and sinners, us sinners, all sinners. God in His almighty power could have just annihilated us sinners – no contest at all! But that God did not want! In His grace, His undeserved love for us, He wanted us to be with Him instead of being against Him or not being at all. So He acted

– He came as God the Son, came for peace. It required that He take our place on the battlefield, not as a resister, but as the conquered One, helpless in the face of God's anger because of all the attacks by us sinners, for that's what our sins are: attacks against God. Could God in His grace just have forgotten about our sins, just not held them against us at all, just immediately forgotten them? No, because God is just and holds Himself to justice. Sin must be punished – suffering must be experienced before peace could be declared.

But we sinners couldn't survive, if we had to suffer as we deserve. So God Himself took our place. In a sense, God punished Himself so that He would not have to punish us. That is how He established peace, the peace between Himself and us. So did Jesus, God the Son, come – so did He establish peace for us.

In arrogance our sinful nature insists on saying: but He didn't have to – He could just have ignored what we do wrong. But that would never have produced peace. For what happens when parents never hold a child responsible for doing wrong? What happens when a criminal is just set free, perhaps with a warning, but no real consequences experienced? That child and that criminal don't change – the child just keeps acting selfishly or meanly or greedily, because there have been no consequences. And the criminal keeps assaulting more and more victims. To just ignore sin is to increase it, not end it. So God acted upon Jesus, giving Him all the consequences of our sinning so that peace could be established between us sinners and Himself.

But how can that work? Someone else suffers for what I have done? I haven't suffered any consequences so why not just keep on sinning?

But something does happen – at least in some sinners. Most sinners, true, do respond with the just-keep-on attitude. But in some this peace process carried out by Jesus first humbles and then comforts and then changes that sinner. This good news message – we call it the "Gospel" – works peace in the heart. It works to change attackers into followers. It changes rebellious children into His sons and daughters who try to work with Him and for Him instead of fight against Him. Won't be changed 100%, because the sinful nature still remains in this life. But this message keeps working so that there is peace in spite of daily "accidents" – although sometimes our attack is no accident but a deliberate effort by the sinful nature to gain control again. Still, the message: But I've established peace through My Son's suffering for you, this message works to overcome the "accidents" or the loss of control "deliberates", and peace resumes.

Jesus came for peace, and He still comes to us for peace. That's what His message is all about. That's what His actions all through that first Holy Week, especially on that Friday, Good Friday, were all about. And as we keep hearing that message in our own minds, peace more and more controls us: we live more and more for Him instead of against Him.

And as that peace works in us, it shows through us so that we can work to live in peace with others more and more, at least with the people with whom we have contact day by day. And we also can become one of those "peacemakers" whom Jesus said are "blessed" (Matthew 5:9).

Grace – mercy – and peace – because of Jesus!

March 24, 2015

Theme: **Maundy Thursday**
Related Reading: 1 Corinthians 11:23-32
Text: Matthew 26:26-28

HIS BODY – HIS BLOOD

Have you ever wondered what that first Maundy Thursday evening was like? Very likely you have the idea, which I used to have, that it was a very serious and solemn occasion. After all, it marked the dividing of the religious history of God's people. There was the Old Testament Passover sacrament, which now was coming to its end, because here was the beginning of the New Testament sacrament of Holy Communion, the new covenant; so, it must have been quite a pious, filled-with-awe night, right?

But it wasn't! Both because that was not the character of the Passover meal and because, realistically, the disciples didn't really understand that the "new" was now beginning. They understood something was happening, but like a number of other teachings of Jesus, they didn't understand much about this new sacrament until after Jesus had ascended into heaven and the Holy Spirit had come to them in that special Pentecost way. So, especially since even we find it so hard to understand and believe that Jesus' Body and Blood are truly and really, physically yet supernaturally, present in/with/under the Bread and Wine (to use a traditional Lutheran phrase which essentially means only "somehow"), we surely can understand that the disciples that night didn't understand, although they remembered.

We also should realize the character of the Passover observance. Yes, it did include a specific ceremony in which a younger person, usually a child, asked in a formal way why the family ate this meal as it did; but it truly was a festival meal with a lot of talking, as happens at family mealtimes, not just religious discussion, but general, even light-hearted, conversation.

And think of what happened at that particular Passover observance on what we call Maundy Thursday. After they all got into their places – which very likely involved some good-natured teasing about who would recline where (since they didn't sit at a table as the famous Leonardo DaVinci painting depicts – they reclined on low couches, resting on one elbow, as was the custom at that time), there came a somewhat embarrassing moment.

Because no one had volunteered to wash everyone's feet, which was also the custom, but was rather humiliating, because that was usually a servant's job, since no one volunteered, Jesus did it. Peter objected, as we know, but didn't say: Lord, let me do that. So it took a while for Jesus to wash the feet of all of them in their embarrassed silence – and to then explain why He did it: you are not to be bosses in My kingdom, but to humbly serve one another and all the others.

Then they began eating, at least having some appetizers; for it was at this time that Jesus warned them all that one of them would betray Him. In the commotion of refusing to believe this and saying: not me, this is when Jesus had the brief conversation with Judas which showed that Judas was the one – however no one apparently noticed this, since they had been reacting against the very idea of a betrayal – nor were they surprised when Judas up and left their meal – they heard Jesus say: Go on, do it quickly, but they probably thought it had to do with going out to take care of something which apparently he had forgotten to do for this Passover time. So, Judas left. And they began to eat the main meal -- remember, it was a regular meal, however with the Passover ceremony included.

After a bit Jesus called for their attention and, when getting it, took a flat, pan-sized piece of unleavened bread, began breaking it into pieces, and said: Take and eat – this is My Body – given for you – do this in remembrance of Me. Which was a shocking statement: after, all, how could it be His Body, when He was there in His body reclining with them – they knew He was handing bread to them, yet He said: This is My Body – what? How can that be? So, undoubtedly Jesus had to repeat what He said even a number of times to be sure they remembered the words, even if they couldn't understand the meaning.

Then they resumed eating the Passover meal, because Luke (21:20) – and also Paul in 1 Corinthians 11 (v.25) – says that toward the end of the meal, "after the supper" are the words used, Jesus took the cup of wine, which had been part of the Passover ceremony and said, as in our text: "Drink from (this) all of you. This is My Blood of the covenant, which is poured out for you for the forgiveness of sins." Again, they had to be mystified by these words: it's wine, not blood; His blood? But He isn't bleeding into this cup. So, again, Jesus must have repeated these words also, as He had about the bread being His Body (which would explain why the words are somewhat different in each account), so they would at least know He really meant it and so they would remember these words, even though again they did not understand them.

"This is My Body...this is My Blood" – it wasn't until afterward, after Jesus' ascension and after the Holy Spirit especially entered them on Pentecost, 50 days after Jesus' resurrection, that they began to understand and began to observe this new ceremony, this new covenant of God, in order to especially remember by His very touch what He did and why He did it, not only for everyone, but for each of them individually.

We, of course, live in that "afterward". It is no easier to understand how the bread we eat and the wine we drink, how these physical things can actually somehow be His Body, His Blood. In fact, it is impossible to understand – but we believe it, because He said it. And in this "afterward" time, because we have the written Word of God to teach us, we can understand what it means for us. It means: we truly are forgiven for all our sins – we individually are forgiven – not by the eating and drinking, but by what He did: gave His Body – this Body, shed His Blood – this Blood, under the punishing wrath of God against our sins. So, because of what He did, we are forgiven! Our sins have been removed from God's sight forever! When? Only now as we "do this" which Jesus commanded? No! Instead, when He did it on the cross on that bleak day we call "Good Friday"! We remember: He did it then! He truly did it – for me!

And because He says: "This IS My Body, My Blood", we know and believe that He still is with us, even as He has promised: "I am with you always, to the very end of the age" (Matthew 28:20), with us, not only assuring us of our having been forgiven, but especially to help us in our living for Him. This we believe, this we know, especially as we do this blessed action "in remembrance of (Him)".

April 1, 2010

Theme: **Good Friday**

Related Reading: Isaiah 53:1-12

Text: John 19:17-18

HIS CROSS

The cross! Such an ugly thing! Such a cruel thing! Why would anyone want to wear it as beautiful jewelry? Not, of course, because of its appearance, but because of its meaning! It was the tool God used to carry out His plan to rescue sinners, us sinners, from what we have earned by our sinning: eternal death.

In the natural order of things once perfection had been ruined by Adam and Eve, physical death was inescapable for sinners, unless God made a special exception to take a person directly into eternal life, the "special exceptions" being a man named Enoch in the time before the flood and the prophet Elijah much later, the only ones we know of from all of history, although at the end of history those who trust in Jesus then will not experience death, but will be gathered before God's throne immediately. But, otherwise, death is inescapable, because "the wages of sin is death" says Romans 6 (v.23), and we have all sinned – so we will all die.

As Jesus had to die! For He was responsible for the sin debts of everyone! Our sinning is like using a credit card: every sin another charge entry – day after day, year after year, big ones, small ones, no matter, all charged to our credit card. Except! God changed the rules! God shifted accounts so that everything we do wrong has been – in His sight – charged to Jesus' account! In 2 Corinthians 5 Paul explains it this way: "God was reconciling the world to Himself in Christ, not counting men's sins against them" (v.19). And Who had to pay? "God made Him Who had no sin to be sin for us so that in Him (Jesus) we might become the righteousness of God" (v.21).

A different way of doing business! God's spiritual way! In order to be able to accept us, He shifted our sin debts to Jesus' credit card. And there on the cross Jesus paid up! Actually, there on the cross was only final payment! All His life Jesus was piling up credits – His perfect life was the line of credit, His suffering and death was then the payment, the complete payment for all sins ever done. For when Jesus said the word which we traditionally translate as: "It is finished!" (John 19:30), He actually spoke in Hebrew which in Greek is a single word which means: Paid! *Tetelestai!* Like stamping a bill: PAID!

That is the meaning of the cross: His life of perfection had led to the cross so He could say: Paid! Done! Completed! And in effect Jesus says: Now that the sins have been paid for, paid in full, all sinners can use My perfect life of righteousness as their ticket into eternal life! And you are using My perfect life and My suffering and death payment, as you trust I did it for you. Because of that meaning is why we value the cross: now it is the symbol of His rescuing us from eternal death for eternal life!

Which is why we use the cross: on display in our church

chancels, as jewelry as reminder to ourselves and as witness to others: He had to and He did all that had to be done for me, for you; which is why many also have the practice of crossing themselves in worship, in prayer – as reminder: Jesus died on the cross for me!

The cross, however, is not merely to be seen or to be worn; it is also to be lived. Our text says that Jesus carried His cross out to the place of crucifixion. Actually, when it got too much for Him physically because of His human physical weakness, another helped, Simon of Cyrene – not willingly – he was forced to do it according to Mark 15 (v.21). In a way, Simon can be a symbol for us and the cross Jesus calls us to carry, the cross of suffering which those who reject and despise Jesus as Savior direct against us. It isn't easy to endure being despised, being ridiculed, being possibly even physically harmed because of our trust in Jesus. But, when we think of how He accepted the cross of our sins and endured all that suffering, we are willing to be faithful to Him no matter how anyone reacts against us because of our faith, because of our faithfulness. Yes, we may not only wear a cross – we will also carry the cross which others impose on us in their hatred for Jesus, He Who gave Himself even for them, paid also for their sins.

The cross! The symbol of all Jesus did to rescue us for eternity! The cross! Never our burden – always our comfort, our witness, our power!

April 26, 2010

Theme: **Easter**

Related Reading: Matthew 28:1-10

Text: Colossians 3:1-4

HIS RESURRECTION – OUR LIVING!

Alleluia! Christ is risen! He is risen indeed! We praise Him!

However, on that first Easter morning absolutely no one, no one – except the One, God Himself, but no human being had any idea about what was going to happen that early Sunday morning! Because everyone was convinced Jesus was dead, dead like any other human being, dead! And done!

The disciples were convinced of that – and even if any had a faint remembering of Jesus having said: In three days I'll rise from the grave, those thoughts were overwhelmed by grief and fear. Oh, the chief priests remembered those words, didn't believe them, of course, but lest the disciples come to steal the body and claim a resurrection, they had a guard posted just to make sure no one came near that dead body. And the women that morning? They above all were convinced Jesus was dead – for they came to embalm a dead body! Yes! He had died! He was dead! And done for!

But then? First the women saw and believed: Arisen! But the disciples refused to believe them – even after they found the tomb empty! Their attitude was: "some of our women ... told us they had seen a vision of angels", but who can believe hysterical women was their implication (Luke

24:22-24). Why their skepticism? Because He was dead and gone – just like any other man!

For that is what the disciples really experienced when they lived with Jesus: a man, just like them, although with extraordinary powers and without any sinning. But still, a man – and His death proved that!

Which is the first reason why Jesus' resurrection was so important, in fact, was essential. As Paul wrote to the Romans: "(Jesus) as to His human nature was a descendant of David and Who through the Spirit of holiness was declared with power to be the Son of God by His resurrection from the dead" (1:3-4), His resurrection proved to the disciples that Jesus was more than just a man – He was actually God as well as human! They had kind of believed that until His dying had confused them. But His resurrection proved: God as well as man, absolutely the promised One! Absolutely!

Now we have to realize that they still on that first Easter – and even for fifty more days – did not understand the "Why" of His being God and man on earth. It wasn't until the Holy Spirit enlightened them on Pentecost that they understood - and believed - that His life and death on earth with all that happened, especially His suffering and dying, was God's plan and action to give forgiveness of sins to sinners. Then they finally could also realize that Jesus' resurrection was proof that what He had done was sufficient and accepted by God's justice so that when He said:

"Finished" on the cross, He didn't mean He had finished drinking from that sponge full of sour wine, but that His work was finished! Completed! Done! Forgiveness had been won! And now was available free for each one who trusted in what He had done, which is our comfort and our joy even on this day! Not just the fact that He rose to life again, but that He truly is our Forgiver, our Savior! Alleluia! He is risen indeed! We praise Him!

Which brings us to our text. For we really cannot feel the emotions the disciples felt that first Easter Day – we have known all along that His death would lead to His resurrection and to the forgiveness of our sins. That is a knowing and a trusting, not an excited feeling. Still, we are to have a continual reaction, a living reaction, to the fact of Jesus' resurrection – which is spelled out in our text: "Since, then, you have been raised with Christ, set our hearts on things above, where Christ is seated at the right hand of God. Set your minds on things above, not on earthly things. For you died and your life is now hidden with Christ in God." (There is a kind of P.S. to this, which we'll think of in a bit.)

What God is teaching us by these words is that when Jesus died, we – in the sense of our sinful nature – also died. That is, our sinful nature is as good as dead in us. We have to put it that way, because we all know by on-going experience that our sinful nature is not totally dead – and gone. Too easily and too often it makes its ugliness known to us inwardly and to others visibly, and this reality will not change until our sinful nature is completely destroyed when we enter eternal life. Then we will live completely according to God's plan and command. Until then, however, there is this struggle.

But what comforts and encourages us is that the absolute power of the sinful nature has been broken; for when Jesus took all our sins to the cross, He won the victory over sin so that we cannot be forced to sin by the devil. It is as James wrote: "Resist the devil, and he will flee from you" (4:7). Not with just the snap of our fingers, of course. But as we use the power of God's Word and the strength the Holy Spirit gives us through the message of Holy Communion that He will help us, we don't have to give in – with the result that eventually the devil does give up – at least in that particular temptation. In this sense, our sinful nature is powerless over us, dead, and the temptations we experience are kind of its death rattles which trouble us.

It does take our conscious effort, however, as the text says: "Set your hearts on things above...set your minds on things above, not on earthly things". And in the verses after our text Paul writes very specifically about what to keep away from (he says: "put to death" this sinning) and what to "clothe yourselves with". The more we let ourselves think about particular sins, the more they attract us and can become sin by us, as we all have experienced. And so God directs us: keep the good things of My will in mind so that you will aim to do them in daily living.

Of course, it is a challenge – especially as we live in a culture which glorifies the sinful and even sordid things of living – so much entertainment and so much advertizing urges us to think only of this life and to do only what pleases our sinful nature, dying though it is in us. So we need real effort to "set" our hearts and minds on God's action in Jesus for us and His will for us to carry out.

But that is how Easter is meant to affect us: Jesus did not stay in the grave – He arose – He lives – He will help us to want and to more and more do what is pleasing to God and truly is good for us – that is our living reaction to His resurrection!

Now for that "P.S." I mentioned earlier; our text gives us this promise: "When Christ Who is your life (meaning: He is the only way for life eternal, which He gives you and me) appears, then you also will appear with Him in glory".

Easter! Not gloom and doom and death, but life and help and living. We say and sing words of praise. But mostly we live it – because through His resurrection we are set free from the deadly way of living in order to live for Him on the way to that eternal glorious life.

Christ is risen! He is risen indeed! We praise Him by our living!

April 20, 2014

Theme: **Sunday after Easter**

Related Reading: John 20:19-31

Text: Luke 24:36-43

ACTUALLY TOUCHING HIM!

What an emotional day it had been! First, the absolute gloom of despair: He's dead! Then the sneering: Nonsense, women, He can't be alive! Then the glimmer of hope: the tomb truly is empty! Then the excitement: Peter saw Him – as well as these two disciples from Emmaus! And now: Shock! And fear! He is standing right here! But, can't be! The doors are all locked (John 20:19) – no way in – but there He is! No! Can't be! A ghost!

Those were the emotions the disciples felt in our text: "They were startled and frightened, thinking they saw a ghost." For no one in a body could have entered that room with no door open – just suddenly! Yet, there He is!

So Jesus speaks lovingly: "Peace be with you." Don't be afraid – it's really Me. "Touch Me and see; a ghost does not have flesh and bones, as you see I have." And to prove this even more: See, I can eat physical food, which no spiritual ghost could do! Yes, it really is Me! Alive! In My actual body! Then "the disciples were overjoyed when they saw the Lord", reports John (20:20). Words are assuring, but the physical touch means so much more – and in this situation was proof. Would that we could so touch Jesus!

Oh, we do have His Word – which makes sense, when

we think about it. For we are sinners – no doubt about that, and His Word says so, too. And we can't make up for our sinning – as His Word also tells us; Galatians 3 explains it this way (v.10): "Cursed is everyone who does not continue to do *everything* written in the Book of the Law" – so, once you have not done "everything", it is then impossible to do "everything", which means that you can't make up for even one sin. None of us can!

However! God does not leave us sinners in that lost hopelessness, for His Word teaches: "But now a righteousness from God, apart from Law, has been made known...This righteousness from God comes through faith in Jesus Christ...all have sinned and fall short of the glory of God and are justified by His grace through the redemption that came by Christ Jesus. God presented Him as a sacrifice of atonement through faith in His blood" (Romans 3:21-25) so that "a man is justified by faith apart from observing the Law" (v.28).

Now this is truly good news for us sinners, isn't it? This gives us peace, doesn't it? We can't save ourselves from God's punishment which we deserve, but He has saved us through Jesus, as He lived and suffered and died for our sins. It doesn't seem fair – from our human viewpoint: He has suffered, while I go free? And not only I, but everyone who trusts in what He has done no matter what they have done? Doesn't seem fair, but it does make sense, even from our human point of view. So, we believe it, don't we?

Yes, except that sometimes we can wonder. Maybe you never do, but I do – and I suspect many of you also – at times. Such wondering, doubt, really, can happen for a number of reasons, but often happens when we are really feeling guilty about our sinfulness. Does He really forgive me – after what I've done – again! Yes, His Word says so, but how can I be sure?

And in our guilt Jesus says: Touch Me – to be sure – that I know what you did – all that you have done – and that I did everything I did – for you – as well as all other sinners! Touch Me! Because a personal touch can assure better than mere words.

But how can we touch Jesus, actually touch Him? The disciples could – and did; even Thomas, that great doubter, did – eventually. But that was then, when He stood before them, back to life in His physical body! But now? He is not here on earth in His physical body any more – He's ascended into heaven! So, how can I touch Him? Impossible!

However! He has said (Matthew 26:26,28): "*This* is My Body...*This* is My Blood", as He gave His disciples a special ceremony, not for them only, but for all those who would trust Him as Savior, so special a ceremony that we call it a "sacrament", a sacred deed, given and done by Jesus for us sinners. Of course, this, too, is a matter of words to believe, for, after all, how can a bit of bread actually be His body, a sip of wine actually be His blood? And yet, if He has said so, why not? Human thinking says: Impossible – if it really were even just a microscopic bit in each bite, in each sip, Jesus' original body and blood would be all used up – gone – by now! So, human thinking says: Jesus must have meant this "represents" His body, His blood – only way it makes sense! But Jesus said: "This IS...this IS!" And unless you are a squirming politician, "is" means "is"! So, somehow this IS His Body, His Blood, so that in this sacrament, which we have named "Holy Communion", we actually touch Jesus! Or, more accurately, He comes and touches us!

For what purpose? Some, many, say: "to forgive you your sins". But in which passage does God's Word make that promise? When Jesus said "This is", He said: "given *for* you...poured out *for* you" (Luke 22:19-20). He did not say: given *to* you or poured out *on* you for the forgiveness of your sins. Nowhere does the Bible say that! The Bible says we receive forgiveness, the forgiveness that was earned for us, when He did give His Body and did pour out His blood – we receive that forgiveness through faith in Him and what He did then! We are forgiven through faith – because of what Jesus *did*, not because of anything that we now do!

Well, what good, then, is this sacrament for us? What does it mean? What is actually happening? It is Jesus' very special assurance to us, His telling us by deed, by touch, that what He did back there on that cross, back then so long ago, was done, not just for "us", for sinners in general, but was done for "you" – as an individual – was done for you personally, you with all your sins, not just those which might be troubling you with guilt at the moment, but for all your sins so you don't have to worry about them, you can let them go, let the guilt go, be at peace. In Holy Communion Jesus personally touches you – and me – to say: I know you – I know all you have done – so remember: I did what I did – for you! Which touch assures us even more than the words, for His touch makes it personal for you!

So, should you and I receive His Body and Blood only when we are feeling especially guilty? No, because, for one thing, we always are guilty, even when we don't particularly feel it. But even more, Jesus' touch means: Not only did I do this so that your sinning doesn't take you away from Me, but also I did this so that you can live for Me. For when I took away your sins there on the cross, I also removed their power over you! I set you free! So you don't have to continue in your sinning, but can live My way, which will please both Me and you. Of course, I know you won't be able to completely in this life – that's why I always want you to remember – especially by means of this sacrament - what I did in this life: took care of all your sins. And by touching you, I am encouraging and strengthening you to follow in My way, as you live each day.

Actually touching Him? It is a mater of faith, true. But what a comfort – and what a power – the touch of His Body and His Blood is!

April 15, 2012

Theme: **Good Shepherd Sunday**

Related Reading: John 10:11-16

Text: Luke 13:31-35

THE FOX – THE HEN – THE CHICKS!

Jesus as the Good Shepherd! We all know and appreciate that description of Jesus. It speaks of His strength, His tenderness, especially His love in that He laid down His life for us sinners. But what about this description of Jesus: Jesus as Mother Hen! Not so appealing to us, doesn't give us much confidence, in fact, even seems somewhat disrespectful. And yet, that's how Jesus refers to Himself in our text: "How often I have longed to gather your children together as a hen gathers her chicks under her wings" – Jesus as Mother Hen!

With good reason! For why and when does a mother hen spread her wings to shelter her chicks? When they are in danger – when a hawk, perhaps, is circling overhead, ready to swoop down to carry off a little chick! Then the clucking: Come, come, little ones, come to safety! At the risk of her own life! For if it is an eagle, that big a bird could dive down and snatch the hen herself! Or, perhaps, a fox is lurking – then the hen does sacrifice herself to try to protect her chicks, for a mother hen would be no match for a fox at all! Yet she would give her life to protect her chicks!

Which sounds very similar to the "Good Shepherd" description, doesn't it? Except that the "Good Shepherd", though willing to give His life, has the strength to beat off the fox or the wolf or even the lion – that's why Psalm 23 says that the shepherd's "rod" is a comfort; for, while the shepherd's "staff" was the guiding and the pull-from-danger tool, his "rod" was his club to beat off animal attackers. But the mother hen has no strength to resist, only the willingness to sacrifice herself, only the desire to protect her chicks.

However, there are some other differences when applying these two descriptions to Jesus and His work for us. First, as the Good Shepherd Jesus willingly did sacrifice His life for us sinners. Yet this was not in a fight with the spiritual lion, the devil, (so described in 1 Peter 5) nor "that fox", Herod (as described in our text). Jesus was strong enough to beat them off, when they threatened Him. Herod, "that fox", wanted to kill Jesus, reported the Pharisees – you see, not all the Pharisees were enemies of Jesus, some were listening to and believing Him. Why did Herod want to kill Jesus? The human reason was that he thought Jesus must be a re-incarnated John the Baptist, who had made him feel so guilty (Matthew 14:1-12) and whom he had killed not too long before our text; so Herod wanted to get rid of any reminder of his guilt – that was the human reason.

But the spiritual reason was that the devil wanted to kill Jesus and was trying to use Herod as his tool to do this. Why? Because the devil was doing all he could to ruin God's plan to rescue sinners from their deserved doom of being his slaves forever in the misery of hell. And the devil thought: if I can get this Jesus killed, then God has lost and I have won! It was beyond his understanding that Jesus' death was part of the plan – actually no one could understand that before it happened, not humans nor angels, good or evil angels – it was God's mystery. The other attack by the devil on God's plan was to get Jesus to sin – that would have ruined the plan, if he had succeeded.

But Jesus, the Good Shepherd, fought off all these attacks. He refused to give in to temptation – He even somewhat ridiculed this attempt to kill Him: tell that old fox that I will do what I must do and he won't and can't stop Me!

Which was as it had to be: Jesus would willingly give His life, when the time and the manner was right according to God's plan, and no one could force Him into premature death. The fox – Herod – and the lion – the devil – would not win! Jesus beat them off every time they attacked, whether temptation to sin or attempt to kill.

Until it was time! Time for what? For God's justice to be done! For that was why Jesus, God on earth, suffered and died: "to demonstrate (God's) justice at the present time, so as to be just and the One Who justifies (those who have) faith in Jesus" (Romans 3:20). For God is not a namby-pamby kind of doddering old grandpa, who just overlooks every wrong thing done. God is the God of justice! Sin must be punished – must be! No exceptions! Yet His love over-rides His justice in that He found the way to punish every sin yet not punish the sinner! That is why He came – God the Son came – and became human, the man, Jesus, so that according to God's plan His justice would be carried out so sinners could be spared.

So Jesus came to suffer and die at the time of God's choosing. Which time was on a Passover Friday outside the city of Jerusalem with its temple altar for sacrifices. Jesus willing sacrificed His life on the altar of the cross, raised up as the shield between the wrath of God's justice and the guilty sinners hiding in His shadow! Actually, of course, Jesus worked out justice for all sins, for all sinners; but the only ones who benefit are those sinners who come to faith in Him as Savior. So did the Good Shepherd lay down His life for us sinners. And we benefit as we trust in what He did as having been done for us individually.

The Mother Hen description of Jesus, however, focuses on another need of us sinners; as Jesus said (v.34): "O Jerusalem...how often I have longed to gather your children together as a hen gathers her chicks under her wings, but you were not willing!" With these words, which He repeated in Matthew 23 (vv.37-39), Jesus is lamenting how He had been trying to call the people away from the false religion which had become the belief of the Jews, the false religion which depended on rituals and sacrifices and outward appearances instead of looking to the fulfillment of God's promises to send the Messiah, Whom whey were to rely on for their eternal welfare. But most of the Jerusalem people were caught up in the outward show of religion and couldn't be bothered about that country hick from Galilee called Jesus, no matter what He taught or how many miracles He did in fulfillment of the prophecies. How sad Jesus was to see such unbelief. He wanted to rescue them – He wanted to shelter them from God's wrath upon their sinning; but they felt they were plenty good enough for God, like that Pharisee who prayed in the temple: "God, I thank You that I am not like all other men" (Luke 18:9-12). How spiritually sad! How eternally tragic!

And what does this mean for us, us sinners living so many centuries later, us sinners who have come to faith in Jesus? We are always in spiritual danger – the devil has not given up in trying to ruin God' plan for us individually. God wants us to be safe for all eternity. And the Holy Spirit has started us on the path of faith which will finally lead to eternal life. But there are so many temptations against faith, primarily the same attraction which kept most of the people of Jerusalem away from Him, the attraction of self-righteousness! How easily we listen to our inner whisper: at least I'm not as bad as other people, some other people! And if we do really listen to that whisper, we are not listening to, not depending on Jesus to rescue us from our sins.

So Jesus keeps clucking like a mother hen – but we call it preaching: Come, little ones, come, My children, come to Me daily. Listen to Me, not to your pride. Listen to Me and hide yourself under the shadow of My arms spread wide on the cross. For only as you are depending on Me to cover over your sins are you protected from the judgment of My justice against your sins. Turn always from what you think you have done to depend on what I have done for you. Trusting in Me, you are safe! Forever!

The picture of Jesus as Mother Hen is not a picture of Him as being defenseless or even as sacrificing Himself for us. Jesus as Mother Hen emphasizes that He provides the eternal protection we need from the consequences of our sinning.

This is why we must hear His continual call through His Word preached to us – so we will trust in His having laid down His life for us as the Good Shepherd. In that faith we stay under His protection. And being His little "chicks", we also try to stay in His "shadow", in His way of life, day by day. *April 22, 2012*

Theme: **Confirmation**

Related Reading: 1 Timothy 1:15-19

Text: Revelation 2:10b

DAD, HOW DO YOU KNOW?

For your confirmation day

My dear granddaughter:

I originally wrote this letter because your dad asked me to write something like this, which he could give to your brother, when he was to be confirmed. As I wrote it, I thought I would like to give it to each of my grandchildren, when they were confirmed. You are now the fourth grandchild to receive it.

When your dad was about your age, one day he asked me something like this question (by the way, your aunt and your uncle had also asked me this in their own words before they were confirmed): "Dad, how do you know that all this we are supposed to believe is actually true?" I wouldn't be surprised if you've wondered the same thing.

Here's how I answered each of them: "I <u>don't</u> know!" Which kind of surprised them, I think – as maybe it surprises you right now. So this is how I explained it.

"If I <u>knew</u> it was true – if it could be proven that it was true, it wouldn't be <u>believing</u> any more." For example, do you <u>believe</u> that two plus two equals four or do you <u>know</u> it? On the other hand, do you "know" that the sun is about

93 million miles from the earth or do you "believe" this? You have to "believe" it, since you haven't actually measured that distance to "know" for sure – although we do have good evidence to "believe" it.

So, we cannot actually "know" for sure that God Himself exists – no one can prove that He does – but also, no one can prove that He doesn't exist. Each person has to "believe" one way or the other. It is "believing" either way, not "knowing".

The same thing regarding the question: will we exist forever or is this life all that will be? There is no proof either way – a person "believes" we will or "believes" we won't.

And the same regarding Jesus as the Savior: if you believe God exists and that you will exist forever, then what do you believe about how you can be with God forever? Will it be because of what you have to do to meet God's requirements *or* will it be because God just automatically takes everyone into eternal life *or* is it because Jesus has done what is necessary for God to accept us sinners? Which will you believe? Remember, no one can "prove" any of these three options in order to "know for sure" – it is strictly a matter of "believing".

So, why "believe" that God does exist and that we will exist forever, either with Him or apart from Him? And why "believe" Jesus is the way to be with God forever after this life?

It's because of that message about Jesus. We all have to admit that we do wrong, that we sin. For sin is not only the terrible things some people do like murder and beating people up and robbing and horribly abusing little children. Sin is also the kind of "little" wrongs we do like telling a lie or cheating on a test or yelling at someone when you are angry or making fun of someone or calling your brother a nasty name or skipping church – all the things we do which are wrong, even if it seems that no one gets hurt very much by that wrong which we do, all of these are also sin.

Most people think – and try to believe that they can make up for those "little" wrong things or that God doesn't really notice such "little" wrongs. But they can only "try to believe" this, because inwardly they feel uneasy about this (that inner feeling is actually the conscience we all have, which tells us we've done wrong or thought wrong).

But the message about Jesus says: because you can't make up for the wrongs you do – not the "little" ones or the "big" ones, Jesus has done what is necessary so that God can forgive them all (not hold those sins against a person), and therefore welcome sinners into eternal life. This message says that Jesus, God's Son come to earth, had to live a perfect life without sinning even once, because we can't live without sinning, and also had to suffer and die to make up for all the sinning that we do.

Is this true? No one can prove it is or it isn't – it's a matter of "believing" it or not.

But why "believe" it is true?

I "believe" it, because when I think about the wrongs I do and then think about this message, it makes sense – and it gives me "peace", that is, I can relax and not worry about the wrongs I've done, because Jesus has taken care of them for me. I've not found any other message which can do this for me.

Of course, I have to add something about what happens when a person actually does "believe" this message about Jesus. Some people say they "believe in Jesus" and that their sins are forgiven, but then think: so I can just do whatever I please, because if I do wrong, it is always forgiven, so it doesn't matter what I do.

But that idea shows no thanks to God for all Jesus did to make up for our sins and shows that the person doesn't actually "believe" in Jesus at all. When we actually *believe* ("have faith" means the same thing) that Jesus has done everything to make up for our wrong-doing, we automatically are thankful for what He did for us, and we show our thanks by trying to do the right things instead of the wrong things. We "try" means: we know we never can do everything completely right, for we will do something wrong every day until we die; but we want to and try to do what Jesus says is right and what is good, because we are thankful to Him.

Showing your faith in Jesus by trying to do what is right

and good will affect your whole life, of course, in whatever you decide to do with your life. God has given you special abilities and wants you to use them, not selfishly just to make money for yourself, but to help other people in their needs. So you can do this in almost any job or career you choose, as long as you have the attitude of wanting and trying to be helpful to other people. You also do this as you live your daily life apart from whatever job you have. Showing your faith doesn't happen just in church. Mostly it happens as you live day by day.

Not that everyone will like you for having this faith and trying to live this way. Those who "believe" otherwise will oppose you and often try to make trouble for you. To be a follower of Jesus means you have to expect to "bear a cross" for Him, meaning: at times you may have to suffer from what others who believe differently will do to you or say about you. That's just the way it is when we believe in Jesus as our Savior and Leader (and you can't have Him just as "Savior" without having Him also as your "Leader" in life – letting Him lead you is showing your thanks to Him for what He has done to save and forgive you).

So far, what I've written sounds like all of this is up to your decision, whether you will believe in Jesus, keep on believing in Him, and try to live for Him. And that's how it *feels* to us. However, Lutherans believe from the Bible that it isn't really us doing this – it is the Holy Spirit Who works in us to cause us to decide for Jesus (but if you ever decide against Him, that truly is *your* decision and *your* fault). But the Holy Spirit can work in us only through the message about Jesus as our Savior. That's why it is essential for us to keep hearing that message each day in personal devotions and each week in a worship service. Of course, the Holy Spirit also works in us through the message which comes to us in Holy Communion; but even then He works only as we are thinking about the meaning (the message) of Holy Communion, which is: Jesus gave His Body and His Blood to take away all my sins which I have done and ever will do – and through that message the Holy Spirit is also giving us help to show our thanks for Jesus better as we live day after day.

I pray, granddaughter, that you will always "believe" in Jesus in the way I have outlined in this letter to you, for then you will see how God blesses and guides you all through your life in spite of any opposition from others, and finally He will bring you into eternal life, where we will see each other again as we live for Him there.

With much love for you – and prayer for you every day,

Grandpa

This is the letter that I have given to each of my grandchildren as they were to publicly confess their faith in the Lutheran ceremony of confirmation.

Theme: **Ascension and After**

Related Reading: Acts 1:1-11

Text: 1 Corinthians 9:24-27

NO PAIN, NO GAIN!

At the ascension of Jesus the disciples were essentially told that they had work to do for Jesus – first they had to wait (until the Holy Spirit came in a special way), but then they had to work. And it would not be easy – there would be pain – for each would have a "cross", whoever followed Him. Our text uses the illustration of athletes to teach that fact.

The big sports thing for me personally in late spring is the NBA playoffs. Not only how two teams will battle so fiercely for 48 minutes so that even a 20-point lead is not necessarily safe, but especially how those men can jump – and dunk the ball! Although I enjoyed playing basketball and wish I still could, I never once in my life dunked the ball – not once! Why? Well, in those distant days it was illegal to dunk, so few tried it. But the real reasons for me were: a. I was proof of the saying that "white men can't jump", and b. I had none of the exhausting training to build up muscles for jumping.

And I am amazed at those training exercises which I've seen nowadays. Exhausting is hardly the word for it! Painful is more accurate! Which proves the saying for most sports: "No pain, no gain!" True now – true also in Paul's time! For, as he writes in our text: "Everyone who competes goes into strict training" with his spiritual application: "I beat my body and make it my slave"! No pain, no gain – true in athletics, but also true spiritually – which the whole idea of bearing one's cross teaches, as Jesus said: "If anyone would come after Me, he must deny himself and take up his cross and follow Me" (Mark 8:34) – what is that other than "no pain, no gain"? As Paul also wrote the Galatians: "Those who belong to Christ Jesus have crucified the sinful nature with its passions and desires" (5:24) – no pain, no gain!

Not that by being strict with ourselves and struggling against ourselves and struggling to do what is right and good, not that our pain results in our gaining the prize of eternal life – Paul uses the athletic training illustration in our text, but his essential teaching is always that eternal life with the forgiveness of our sins is God's gift to us. The prize of eternal life has already been won for us by the struggle, by the pain of Jesus. He truly was crucified for us – He truly suffered the pain we should suffer for our having disqualified ourselves by our sinning – although let's use the word "transgressions" instead of "sins" in this explanation, because "transgression" means: go across the line, that is, go out of bounds, beyond the boundaries of God's Law. In a race if a runner gets off the course, especially taking a shortcut, that runner is automatically disqualified, has lost. In the race of life we have "transgressed" God's way, crossed His line of "no", so we are disqualified by our actions, our transgressions. Except Jesus has come and has substituted for us, run the race of obedience for us and suffered the pain to make up for how we transgress. Truly, Jesus has won the race! And He gives us "the crown which will last forever"! Gives it to us, as we bow our heads in humility to let Him so crown us!

So, why isn't our role now just to sit on the sidelines and cheer? Why aren't we now just the audience shouting praises to honor our teammate Jesus? What's this about our running the race, our bearing the cross, our "no pain, no gain"? If we have it given to us, how and why do we have to struggle with great effort, even pain, to get it? Because we are to be the best teammates we can be for Jesus! His work for us is completed, but our work for Him is continued – as long as we live in this life! And our work for Him is to try to sign up more players for His team!

Yet, that signing up is accomplished only when those other transgressors, the other sinners we know, can see results in us by what we do, by how we live; only then do they listen to the sign-up spiel – to put it light-heartedly – which seriously is: listen to this message, this great news of how Jesus has won the victory and wants to give the prize to those who have lost, those who are lost on their own. Seeing the difference it makes in us is what helps people, other sinners like us, to listen and believe and so join team Jesus! Of course, in all of this the Holy Spirit does the convincing, just as it is the Holy Spirit Who gives us the desire and the power to show that we are the best team members we can be. The Holy Spirit is the One Who makes us able to praise Jesus, the real winner, by our faithful deeds as well as by our joyful words.

So, what is your cross that brings pain to you? Each of us has at least one – each of us has to undergo the "no pain, no gain" fact of spiritual life; if we refuse to suffer whatever pain is involved, we are transgressing totally, turning completely away from team Jesus and the eternal prize He gives us, for although it is given to us as a gift, not as an earning, still the process involves the fact: "no pain, no gain".

When I was a young pastor, I thought that the only real cross we had to bear was the opposition we experienced from unbelievers against our faith. So, I thought, an illness you might have is not really "a cross you had to bear". But I was wrong. The Christian cross can be any suffering you have, physical, emotional, spiritual. For the bearing of your cross is how you react to the suffering you experience. So, the Christian cross can be the threat of death – as Christians in Muslim countries face; or the sneers of unbelievers who claim you believe in a fairy tale (as though evolution isn't a fairy tale nor space-time wormholes as some astronomers have seriously claimed); or the Christian cross might be the selfish marriage partner or children you have or the always criticizing relative or neighbor in your life; or the Christian cross could be the illness or body condition you have with its challenge to be accepting and positive and helping others anyway instead of wallowing in self-pity; or the Christian cross could be an on-going emotional illness you struggle with, an addiction or a particular temptation which so often assaults you – these as well as so many other struggles are Christian crosses. Which one – or ones – has God guided for you to bear?

Whichever cross – or crosses – you have in your life, how can you keep enduring them? How can you "beat (your) body (or your attitudes) (to) make it (your) slave" so you stay in the race for Jesus and not turn away into disqualification? Which can happen to any of us, as Paul even knew about himself, as he writes in our text: "so that...I myself will not be disqualified". It's not an option, folks! Following Jesus does not mean just watching others, just loafing. You either are in the race with all of its pain or you are lost!

So, how to stay in the race to the crown of eternal life which Jesus has given us through faith, but which requires us to make efforts to show we are on that way so others will see and hear and join the team? "No pain, no gain" is in every real effort. Such as: can't be in the race unless we keep hearing His message so we will keep on the only path: faith in Him alone; but this will mean – hearing according to His rule of every week in public worship (if at all possible, no false excuses, please) – which involves the pain of getting up to get to worship instead of sleeping in, instead of playing something else, whether actual playing or just watching, as well as sometimes the struggle, the pain, of paying attention while at worship. Another way is to force oneself to make the time each day to have a personal devotion with Bible reading involved no matter how busy life seems – getting up ten minutes earlier can provide the time – so, will you snore on St. Mattress or read from St. Matthew? Another way is to tell yourself when tempted to transgress in some way: That's wrong – do the right; but also: Lord, help me! Another way is, when dealing with an obnoxious person or someone who has deeply hurt you: But I will do good to this person, not the evil my sinful nature wants in revenge, because Jesus has done good to me and He says: "Do not be overcome by evil, but overcome evil with good" (Romans 12:21). All of these are hard to do, difficult, painful even; but "no pain, no gain", no gain for team Jesus! And in all of these we will pray: Lord, have mercy! Help me do what You want as right and good, no matter how difficult, no matter what my sinful nature wants!

Will these ways work? Will we gain if we so endure the pain? Frankly, not automatically – just as the athlete does not immediately see results – it takes on-going disciplined effort. But eventually the athlete can jump higher and run faster and play longer. Spiritually, we also will gain in faithfulness – as Paul wrote to the Galatians: "Let us not become weary in doing good, for at the proper time we will reap a harvest, if we do not give up" (6:9).

Ashamedly I must confess – as we all must: I don't always use these methods – I shy away from the pain – sometimes. We all do. Which is why Jesus came and won the prize of eternal life for us. Which is, no, HE is why we will keep trying to deny ourselves and take up our cross to follow Him – so others also will.

Theme: **Pentecost**

Related Reading: Acts 2:1-16

Text: Ephesians 1:13-14

HEARING, BELIEVING, PRAISING

Pentecost! Without a doubt Pentecost is the second most important day in the history of the Christian Church. Most important, of course, is Good Friday, when Jesus finished His work of salvation so there could be the Christian Church at all. Some would say that Easter is of next importance, but Easter did not add to His work – Easter only announced that His work had been successfully completed and accepted. But Pentecost is when the Holy Spirit finally provided the explanation of Jesus' work so that sinners believed it, first the 120 disciples who had been waiting and praying and trying to figure out what it all meant, and then on that very day the 3000 more whom the Holy Spirit convinced through Peter's very first sermon. On that first Christian Pentecost day (for the Greek-speaking Jews had called the "Festival of Weeks" or Spring Harvest "Pentecost", since it was 50 days after the Passover), so, on the first Christian Pentecost day the Christian Church formally began.

This working of the Holy Spirit that day was the "baptism of the Holy Spirit" which both John the Baptist and Jesus Himself had promised. And it happened only once – at least in the way it did with rushing wind and tongues of fire. And its whole purpose was to explain and convince. That's why those 120 disciples began to speak in languages which they had never learned, but which the crowd of pilgrims understood: "we hear them declaring the wonders of God in our own native tongues (languages, or, the Greek word is translated more precisely: dialects)!" (Acts 2:11). The human fact is that, unless you are fully fluent in a foreign language, you can much better understand when something is explained in your own native language. What those disciples finally understood and believed and then proclaimed, the Holy Spirit worked through to bring others into that same faith in Jesus as the Promised Savior.

However, we are not to expect that such a dramatic personal experience of the Holy Spirit has to be felt by us. Our text says that the Ephesians had been "marked with a seal, the promised Holy Spirit, Who is a deposit guaranteeing our inheritance". Those who call themselves "Pentecostals" or "charismatics" claim that this "deposit" is expressed by "speaking in tongues", a heavenly language. But that's not what happened on the first Pentecost! The disciples that day spoke in understandable human languages. And later on, Paul instructed that anyone who had been given that special gift, as some were in those early years of the Church, was to use it publicly only if someone was present who could translate what the person was saying (1 Corinthians 14:28). The will – plan – of the Holy Spirit's working is always to have people understand so they can believe. No one can believe if what is spoken is only gibberish!

What, then, is the Holy Spirit as "seal", which is our

guarantee of the eternal "inheritance"? First we have to understand what this "guarantee" means. We sinners would like an absolute guarantee that we will receive eternal life, that we will never fall away and lose that gift – with the unspoken thought that this is guaranteed no matter what we do, no matter how we might sin!

But there is no such guarantee! The so-called "gift" of "speaking in tongues" sure isn't – for look how many publicly-known charismatic men and women have fallen into unbelief through sexual immorality, greed, and/or drunkenness! And those who claim: "but those are only sins" have to listen to God's Word which clearly warns: "those who live like this will not inherit the kingdom of God" (Galatians 5:21). Same for anyone who claims: I'm baptized, so I am guaranteed! If so, why did Paul state his non-guaranteed status not once but at least twice? "Not that I have already obtained all this, or have already been made perfect, but I press on...toward the prize for which God has called me" (Philippians 3:12-14) and "so that after I have preached to others I myself will not be disqualified" (1 Corinthians 9:27). Of course, Paul was confident about receiving the gift of eternal life. But he recognized that he still could fall away. Anyone can fall away from faith! There is no absolute guarantee that we won't!

So, what is this "deposit" of the Holy Spirit which our text is teaching "guaranteeing our inheritance"? What is this being "marked" in Him (Jesus) with a "seal"? It is Baptism! For Baptism is God's pledge to us that we can have "a good conscience toward God" because of the work of Jesus to rescue us sinners for eternal life. How can we have that "good conscience"? By being good enough? Nope! Being "good enough" is not good enough in God's judgment! Completely good – that's the standard! Which is our status before God's justice only by having been washed free of all our sins – past, present, and future – by the blood of Jesus! A "good conscience" is a forgiven conscience – no other possibility! And a "forgiven conscience" is ours only through faith in Jesus as our Rescuer, our Savior.

And – guess where that faith comes from, how do we have it? By the work of the Holy Spirit through the message of the good news about Jesus and His work to rescue us! Remember the first Pentecost? The words had been spoken and thought about by those 120 disciples – the Holy Spirit came – and, finally, they understood – and believed! Peter preached – the Holy Spirit worked – and 3000 believed! "Faith comes from hearing the message, and the message is heard through the word of (preaching about) Christ" (Romans 10:17). Which is also what our text teaches: "And you also were included in Christ when you heard the word of truth, the gospel of your salvation. Having believed (through hearing that message), you were marked in Him with a seal, the promised Holy Spirit". For it always happened that way in the early church: people heard, they believed – and they were baptized. Only a "believer's baptism"? Whole households – including children – were baptized, for example, the prison guard commander in

Philippi (Acts 16 30-33). The Holy Spirit used what the Ephesians heard about Jesus having suffered and died for their sins in order to cause them to believe it! As they were baptized, they were assured the Holy Spirit would keep working to keep them believing – as they kept hearing the gospel message.

So, our guarantee is that as the Holy Spirit used the message to bring us to faith, so He will keep working to keep us in faith as we keep using, that is, hearing and believing, this very message about Jesus.

How essential, then, that we keep hearing the good news about Jesus as our Savior. But don't we know it already? Sure! But we don't always want to keep believing it! Too easily in daily life we get distracted by temptation, not only temptation toward what is evil (those three fatal evils which I mentioned a little while ago which are so much around us in our daily living: sex, greed, drugs); but also we are tempted toward self-righteousness: I'm good – I'm better – I'm safe. So we need God's message: our only hope and rescue is Jesus and what He did for us! Only way! Keep trusting only in Him!

And we also need the continual urging of God's instruction about showing that trust. For trust is not trust if it is only words in one's head. Our text refers to this when it says (not the NIV translation which I usually quote, but this quote from An American Translation, which I am convinced better translates the Greek words here): "That He might free you to be His people and to praise His glory". Our faith, our trust in Jesus, is always to show in our daily living – it can – since we've been freed from slavery to sin and the devil, freed to be able to live God's way – according to His commands, primarily the positive commands, which are summarized in Jesus' words: "Love each other" (John 15:12). But this isn't always what we remember to do in daily life, is it! So God has to remind us from His Word week after week so that through that hearing the Holy Spirit will keep working to keep us living in ways which "praise His glory", ways which show how thankful we are for His having rescued us.

Hearing leads to believing which shows in praising: that's the essential pattern of remaining in faith, in trust, in Jesus, our Savior.   *June 8, 2014*

Trinity

Related Reading: 2 Corinthians 13:11-14

Text: Isaiah 6:1-9

HOLY! HOLY! HOLY!

Probably most of you reading this "Message" have not asked the question about God which I am shortly going to ask, although possibly some of you have, and I'm quite sure it is at least one of the questions atheists have which make them believe there is no "god". The question is: how can God actually have all the qualities – theologically called "attributes" – which we say He has? I mean, as the Bible says in Romans (1:19-20) and Hebrews (3:4), from the creation we live in anyone can rationally see that a "god", Someone or Some Great Force, exists and must have great power. That Someone also must be very wise to have created this very intricately and mutually dependent universe – think of eyesight or even just blood, think of the laws of gravity, etc., which keep the stars and their planets in their fixed positions in relation to each other. Our rational human thinking can conclude at least: Someone – very powerful – very wise.

But the other things that are claimed, at least by those who listen to what the Bible teaches, things such as being everywhere at once (omnipresent) and knowing everything (omniscient), how can that be? I mean, to know every person alive, even down to how many hairs on your head (Matthew 10:30)? Impossible! Says our human thinking!

Or, that He can guide everything that happens, not forcing but guiding – for God's "will" is not absolute but is His "plan" (else no one would ever sin), so, guiding everything for "good" for everyone, at least for all who love Him (Romans 8:28)? Impossible! says our human thinking! Or that this Someone is only one – yet – somehow – has a "threeness" to Him? Three, but not three gods – three but only one God? Impossible! says our human thinking!

But, of course, that is our problem: "our human thinking"! Who are we to judge what God can be or can do? Someone I read long ago said: if we could squeeze God inside the limits of our human understanding, then we would be bigger than God! Yet exactly that is what our human pride wants to do: make ourselves big enough to understand God – and if we can't, then to say like an arrogant college student who thinks he or she knows all the answers to life's problems: Impossible! Can not be! And we all have that kind of arrogance in our sinful nature, still lurking there, ready to challenge God when we want our own way instead of His! After all, that's what sin is, isn't it? Instead, how much we need to have the humility Isaiah was forced into according to our text.

Isaiah had a vision, a stupendous vision of God in about 740 B.C. (year of King Uzziah's death is somewhat uncertain). He saw God in an eternal temple with angels constantly flying around Him and praising Him: "Holy, holy, holy is the Lord Almighty; the whole earth is full of His glory." Now, of course, this was a spiritual vision not a physical reality, for God is Spirit and angels are spirits, yet God made them all appear to Isaiah in ways that he could understand in order to teach him – teach Isaiah what? That God is holy, separate from sin, and Isaiah, a sinner, could have no hope in himself before God: "Woe is me! I am ruined! For I am a man of unclean lips, and I live among a people of unclean lips, and my eyes have seen the King, the Lord Almighty." Realize who you are, Isaiah! No pride possible because of your sinning! No hope in yourself!

But God was actually teaching that sinner Isaiah could have hope, even peace before God because of God's action toward sinner Isaiah. With a live coal from the sacrifice on an altar an angel touched Isaiah's mouth: "See, this has touched your lips! Your guilt is taken away and your sin atoned for." And then the Lord commissioned Isaiah to do His work of warning other sinners and calling them to this same forgiveness so they could also truly serve the Lord.

So the Lord also teaches us: because of sin we should have no hope – but God has provided the way of forgiveness (which we know – after the fact – is through the sacrifice of Jesus on the altar of His cross) so that also we are now qualified to serve God as we live our lives.

Part of the way we serve God is by believing what He has revealed about Himself, believing even when we can't understand. Such as His Three-in-One-ness, His being only One God yet three Persons while still remaining only One. Which is absolutely beyond our understanding! It is in the

New Testament of Scripture that this is revealed so clearly. "Baptizing them in the name of the Father and of the Son and of the Holy Spirit" (Matthew 28:19) is the clearest statement. "May the grace of the Lord Jesus Christ and the love of God and the fellowship of the Holy Spirit be with you all " (2 Corinthians 13:14) is almost as clear. Jesus taught that He was God, when He said: "I and the Father are one" (John 10:30), and if a person lies to the Holy Spirit, he lies to God (Acts 5:3-4). So, Three distinct Persons, yet only one God (Mark 12:29).

But the Old Testament also taught the Three-in-One-ness of God, just not so clearly. Already in the creation it was hinted at: "Let *us* make man in *our* image" (Genesis 1:26). The blessing which Aaron spoke upon the Israelites had three distinct parts: "The Lord bless you and keep you; the Lord make His face shine upon you and be gracious to you; the Lord turn His face toward you and give you peace" (Numbers 6:24-26), and these three statements align quite well with what is taught about the Father being the Creator Who blesses and protects, the Son being the Redeemer Who brings God's grace to us sinners, and the Holy Spirit being the One Who actually works in us so that through faith in what the Son did while on earth we have peace with the holy God, because we are forgiven – which is what Isaiah also realized dramatically in our text when the Lord's action took his guilt away because his sinning had been atoned for by the sacrifice God made. And now, it is also instructive that in our text the angels in this vision call out to one another: "Holy, holy, holy is the Lord Almighty". That triple "holy" could perhaps be merely poetic cadence, but doesn't it also imply: the one "Lord Almighty" has a "three-ness" about Him?

So, the teaching of the Trinity nature of God was quite veiled in the Old Testament. But no more veiled than the exact work of God to atone for the sins of the world by the suffering and death of Jesus. Looking back – after the fact – one can see it taught there: so many prophecies finally were recognized as prophecies and did finally make sense. But in the Old Testament time the people never figured out the details – they only trusted: our God will atone for our sins – somehow. Since we are thinking together about not understanding but still believing, isn't that the faith of the Old Testament believers regarding how God would finally do it? We don't understand how – but we trust He will!

And so when our sinful nature thinking begins to question and to wonder – whether it is about God's nature – as we've been thinking together in these few minutes – or about how God is guiding in our personal lives or in the lives of people we care about or know about (such as someone dear getting an incurable disease or those children killed in the recent Oklahoma tornado: why so random? how can there be "good" in this?), we openly answer ourselves – or others who ask us: we can't understand – but we trust what God says – about Himself – about what He guides or allows to take place – we trust His Word, because we trust His most important message, His "good news" to us sinners:

"This (message about Jesus as Savior) has touched your lips (and heart); your guilt is taken away and your sin atoned for." In that assurance we have peace, even when we cannot understand.

May 26, 2013

Theme: **July 4th**

Related Reading: Romans 13:1-7

Text: Philippians 3:17-21

THE DUAL PATRIOTISM OF A CHRISTIAN

As we come toward the end of our national patriotic holiday, how patriotic were you these past days? Which brings another question: what is being patriotic? The dictionary definition essentially says: showing one's loyalty and support for one's country. Such loyalty and support shows itself in honoring the flag, respecting authority, obeying the laws, and working to improve the conditions and lives of all one's fellow citizens. A person might express that patriotism with the phrase: In spite of its flaws and weaknesses, I'm proud to be an American!

A rather large number of our fellow citizens, however, do not seem to be proud to be Americans: they constantly find fault with and blame our country for all sorts of problems among us and in the world – they seem to want to change our country into being more like some other country, whether socialist (in the extreme sense) or even communist (when the state controls everything). Some of these would say: I'm just trying to "improve" our country. But one does not "improve" something by trying to destroy its basic principles.

Then there is another kind of lack of patriotism, which exists even among some who would claim to be patriotic –

the attitude which God through Paul condemns in our text. He writes it in regard specifically to some who were in the church and claiming faith, but it applies also to those merely claiming patriotism. Paul wrote: "As I have often told you before and now say again even with tears, many live as enemies of the cross of Christ. Their destiny is destruction, their god is their stomach, and their glory is in their shame. Their mind is on earthly things."

Which describes the life-style, it seems to me, of a growing number of Americans. Our culture is becoming more and more coarse, vulgar, and immoral. Party – party – party! Let the liquor flow – and legalize the drugs! And give me more and more things to fill my belly and entertain my eyes! With as little effort on my part as possible! Tax everybody else – but the government owes me - more and more!

These attitudes are anti-patriotic, because they produce weak and irresponsible citizens. History shows that when homosexuality, for example, becomes widely accepted by a country, that country declines and falls. Our text condemns those who "glory in their shame" and says "their destiny is destruction" (although by His grace anyone can be rescued from that destiny if they come to faith which shows in faithful living).

Of course, such destructive living has always been a part of every country to a certain extent. But the whole vulgar, immoral, and materialistic mess seems in our country now to becoming the usual rather than the minority attitude.

In contrast, our text – and the rest of Scripture – calls us to real patriotism. In a sense, we who trust in Jesus as Savior are to practice a dual patriotism. For we are called to sound earthly patriotism, the patriotism of, first, being thankful for the country into which we have been placed (for that's why we were born Americans or have become Americans – it was God's guidance and blessing – although if you are of a different citizenship, you can thank the Lord for that blessing), then, second, being a good citizen of this country. Paul (Romans 13) and Peter (1 Peter 2) make that unmistakably clear – including respect for officials in authority (even if we oppose their policies and activities), paying taxes willingly. Such should be our earthly patriotism.

But even greater is to be our eternal "patriotism": how we live, because we have a greater citizenship than our earthly location. We belong to God and have an eternal future with Him. That is to show and to guide our life in this nation.

We have our earthly citizenship by being born into it or by having passed the requirements to be declared a citizen. We have our eternal citizenship not by virtue of merely being born or on the basis of anything we can do. Instead, we have it because of the cross of Jesus, the only Savior. Born into this world we are automatically contaminated by the sin of this world, which we then also participate in. And that sinning is never far from us. We also so easily can live as "enemies of the cross of Christ" by willingly going along with the evil culture of those around us. With so much "party – party – party" activity with too much to drink or even to eat as well as immoral attitudes around us, we can get drawn into it – if only occasionally. How tempted we can be to measure our lives on the basis of having so many things or vacationing in so many places. But even more dangerous is the lure of selfishness: all for me – my way! No matter how good we are most of the time or in some ways, our sinning keeps us from meeting even the basic requirement of eternal citizenship, the requirement of perfection.

So Jesus came – so Jesus lived – a perfect life. Which perfection was enough to be distributed to each sinner so eternal citizenship could be received. To receive His perfection, however, first we have to be freed from our sin. Which is why He went to the cross. His being God come to earth made Him big enough so all human sinning would be forgiven and all human beings would be given eternal citizenship. Which does not happen automatically, but happens as sinners come to trust, to depend only on what Jesus did: how perfectly He lived, how totally He suffered to cancel out our sins. It is by faith in Jesus that we have that eternal future with God instead of the "destiny (of) destruction" which we deserve.

Which is why we are to be "patriotic" for the eternal

country we will eventually enjoy. This "patriotism" shows itself in how we live day by day, as our text says: "Join with others in following my example and take note of those who live according to the pattern we gave you." Which "pattern" was: to do the right things God has commanded – do what is good for others as well as possible – live with kindness and helpfulness – and be a good citizen of the country – and community – into which God has placed you.

Therefore, we need to make the effort to live in this way – we need to be alert and on guard so we are not misled by the evil-living culture around us – or by the lust active in us – yet always comforted by the good news of God that He does forgive us when we stumble, and He does give us renewed help to resume this godly patriotism.

God has blessed us to live this life in this country. God has blessed us even more to have His eternal "country" waiting for us after this life. As we are doubly "patriotic" in these ways, we can sing: "God bless America", for He will use us to bring blessing to our country.

July 6, 2014

Theme: **Labor Day**

Related Reading: 2 Thessalonians 3:6-13

Text: 1 Thessalonians 4:11-12

WHY GET A JOB?

Why get a job? he asks. Some might reply: Who can get a job these days? And after all, add some, there's food stamps and other programs, so why bother? Such government programs can encourage human selfishness. One can read various reports that a person would have to earn more than $15 an hour (c. $30,000 a year) to just be even with all the government programs a family could qualify for; even worse, the welfare benefits are non-taxable while the $15 an hour job is taxed, so, why get a job? Others, retired, might also think: Why should I even be concerned about having a job? I'm living o.k. on my retirement benefits. Not all are – but most are, so again: Why get a job?

But according to Scripture we all need to work – so wrote Paul to these same Thessalonians to whom our text was written, when he wrote them that second time: "If a man will not work, he shall not eat" (II,3,10).

However, did you notice the change in terminology? In one way there is no difference between working and having a job. Yet, there is a practical difference. A "job" usually means: "working for pay". "Work", on the other hand means (put informally): "expending effort to complete a responsibility" – whether pay is involved or not.

An example – sometimes women will say about themselves: I didn't ever have a job – I was just a housewife. Oh? No work involved in being a housewife? But being a housewife/homemaker/mother is the most important job in the world, because of how that housewife/homemaker/mother influences the people of the household. Real work, important work, involved!

Another example – my surgeon after my hip surgery eight months ago said: your job now for these next months is to recover from this in order to walk normally again – and, believe me, that has involved a lot of effort: work!

Or, as I recently discussed with some residents at the rehabilitation facility, where I'm serving as volunteer chaplain: physical therapy – that's real work, right? And it's also really work at times to act pleasantly in spite of hurting much!

So, what work, what job, do you have right now in your life?

When Paul wrote to the Thessalonians in both letters, he meant, however, the working which produced payment so they and their families would not be dependent on anyone else for their daily needs. Helping others in need also is expected, as Paul wrote to the Ephesians: "He who has been stealing must steal no longer but must work, doing something useful with his own hands, that he may have something to share with those in need" (4:28). So, we should be self-supporting, if at all possible, as well as helping others.

Why? Our text says: "so that your daily life may win the respect of outsiders" (as well as of "insiders", that is, fellow believers, also). For it is just human nature – also in a congregation – to look down on someone who refuses to provide for one's own family. Again, those who truly are in need deserve and have our compassion. But those who just refuse to support themselves and are free-loaders on everyone else are not respected. Instead, work to support yourself and your dependents – that gains you respect from others and from your own conscience, because it is ingrained in us to work – it goes all the way back to Adam in the Garden of Eden: he was supposed to "work it and take care of it" (whatever that involved, but which means, doesn't it, that gardening truly is the world's "oldest occupation" – Genesis 2:16).

It isn't only having a job that wins the respect of others. Our text includes "lead(ing) a quiet life...mind(ing) your own business" as well as "work(ing) with your hands" – which cannot mean that only manual labor is acceptable "work" – if it were, then all the apostles (except Paul, a tent-maker) would have been disobeying God's Word, since the early twelve disciples left their jobs (at least eventually) to be full-time "church workers". And in our day so many jobs are more mental than manual. In Paul's day, however, most jobs were manual so that's what he is commanding.

But, as I illustrated earlier in this "Message", there is more to "work" than just paying "jobs". And this is the primary application of this text to all of us. Each of us needs to "work", that is, use our time and effort in constructive ways. Not that we should never relax to play or find entertainment. But that should not be our main aim or activity in living, even if we should be well-off enough to be able to only so "play". The Lord does not give us continued life to merely play or loaf. He has purpose for us in living, work for us to do. (By the way, don't be surprised to find eventually that we will have "work" to do in eternal life! If Adam had "work" in the first Creation, won't there also be "work" in the new Creation? Scripture does not really teach that all we will do in eternity is stand around and sing!)

There is, however, one kind of work not a single one of us can do or even dare try to do. That is the work of earning our way into God's forgiveness and eternal blessing. Can't be done, because the entry fee is perfection – and none of us is perfect, sinless, so none of us can earn God's blessing. In fact, that would be a contradiction in itself, for a "blessing" is a gift, and a gift cannot be earned – or it isn't a gift but a payment. And God says clearly that all we can earn is the punishment of "death", temporal and eternal; He says: "The wages of sin is death" – while instead: "the gift of God is eternal life in Christ Jesus, our Lord" (Romans 6:23).

Oh, by nature we try to earn our way, try to be good enough for God. But when God looks at our "work record" with daily failures, He has said to each of us, in effect:

117

"You're fired!" Yet He worked out a different way so that He would not have to put us "out of work" forever – in hell, but could give us the "gift of eternal life".

This " gift" is "in Christ Jesus"! Jesus came and lived a perfect life – that's the entry fee. And He paid up all our debts (failures to be perfect, sins) also – by His suffering and dying. And because He was not merely a human being, but was God on earth, His earning and His payment are enough to pay the entry fee for every sinner, no matter how a person has sinned. That is God's message to us.

Which means: we can't pay – we can only receive this gift from Jesus. To attempt to earn our own ticket is to reject Jesus as Savior. To even think that we in even a little way help to pay is to reject what Jesus did. Remember! We've been "fired" from trying to earn it at all. All we can do is to trust that His payment is enough. We call this faith. In effect, we let Him pay our way.

Which puts us in debt to Him – in a different way, of course. We owe it to Him to live as He commands, to work according to the opportunities He gives us. We are not completing the entry fee price by how we live – that would be "paying". Instead, we only respond in thanks for His having paid completely.

Sometimes this way of life is rather easy. We see opportunities to help someone in need, to work at an enjoyable paying job, to be kind to strangers as well as friends – we see these opportunities and do the best we can to carry them out – and it doesn't even seem like much effort. But sometimes it involves great effort – such as to forgive, when we are still suffering from being hurt – or the effort involved when great physical pain is part of life – or the needs of someone else in their illness never let up and you are the only one who can help – effort! Work! Life can be exhausting!

But the Lord gives us as much help as we need to meet our "job opportunities", our work for Him. And part of His help comes as we remember: what I am doing to carry out the responsibilities I have, I am doing to thank Him for how He worked to save me.

Labor Day, a once a year holiday! But for us who have been helped eternally by the labor of Jesus, each day is a "labor day", rather, a "thanks-living day", in which we use the time of each day, not primarily to play, but also constructively, however that might be, as work for our Savior.

August 31, 2014

Theme: **Reformation**

Related Reading: Ephesians 4:1-6

Text: 2 Chronicles 34:29-33

ANOTHER REFORMATION NEEDED

Today many churches around the world are looking back in history to October 31,1517, when a relatively young professor – Luther was 34 at the time – nailed a set of statements for public debate on the doors of the cathedral in Wittenberg, Germany. Nothing special about using the church door – that's how public events were publicized then (because most everyone went to worship and would see a posted notice). Nothing really special either about what Luther intended: he only wanted to debate these "95 Theses", as they were called, with fellow professors and other scholarly people.

Luther did not intend a church-wide "reformation" by requesting this debate – he only opposed what he saw as abuse of the system for people getting forgiveness of their sins in this life and the escape of purgatory punishment. Luther at that time did not reject purgatory. But he was objecting to the sale of "indulgences", documents which claimed that sins were forgiven and sinners suffering in purgatory were being set free from their torments. Essentially Luther was saying: no sinner can buy forgiveness of sins. And he was sure that the pope must not have known this was happening and would not allow it, if he knew. From these "theses" it is evident he did not want to split the medieval church; he merely wanted to correct these specific errors.

What he didn't foresee, however, was that these statements for debate would lead to what became the "Reformation". Especially German governmental rulers were incensed that so much money was being sent out of their lands to the pope for his pet projects. And there was much other anger against the corruption and immorality of so many priests and church leaders. So the 95 Theses became the "spark", and the Reformation was the explosive result. But on Luther's part it was unintentional – and unforeseen.

Far different was the church reformation described in our text. King Josiah had been made king when he was only eight years old (such boy-kings were not unusual – because adult "counselors" could then run the country for their own profit and power and pleasure). But Josiah was an unusual kid; in spite of all the idolatry around him, he "did what was right in the eyes of the Lord and walked in the ways of his father (ancestor) David, not turning aside to the right or the left" (34:2), especially beginning this faithfulness publicly when he was 16 (34:3), which is when he began to take some control as king. He began getting rid of the idols and altars of the pagan gods, which most of the Israelites were worshiping (primarily because of all the free sex offered, most likely). And when he was 26, he really and intentionally started his "reformation".

Ungodly attitudes had gotten so bad that the temple was almost in ruins. Josiah directed that it be repaired. In that reconstruction work a priest found "the Book of the Law of the Lord that had been given through Moses" (34:14) – scholars think it probably was the book of Deuteronomy. After it was read to him, Josiah was even more determined to bring about a "reformation" – which began with the event described in our text: he called the people of Jerusalem together and "read in their hearing all the words of the Book of the Covenant which had been found in the temple of the Lord" (v.30). Then he pledged himself to faithfulness to that "covenant" and commanded all the people to also pledge themselves to it. Which he did not allow to be just a matter of words, but led them into faithful living: he "removed all the detestable idols...and had all who were present in Israel serve the Lord their God" (v.33). Which reformation lasted for about 13 years: "as long as he lived they did not fail to follow the Lord, the God of their fathers" (v.33).

But it didn't last. Soon after Josiah died, the next kings, beginning with his son, turned again to idolatry, which God specifically punished by having them conquered by Nebuchadnezer, who destroyed the temple and took all the remaining people into exile in Babylonia.

And history is always that way: reformations don't last. Sooner or later the devil worms his way into the attitudes of people to turn more and more in the church to despise the God of their fathers, the true God. It happened after Luther's death: many church leaders began teaching their own ideas instead of sticking to God's Word. The Holy Spirit did work, however, to correct those errors in the document which is called the "Formula of Concord", although not all churches which called themselves "Lutheran" agreed to or followed it.

With the result that more and more Lutheran churches have gone away from proclaiming the message of the Bible, the message that Jesus is the Savior and that He is the only Savior available for sinners, the message that Jesus Himself taught: "I am the way, the truth, and the life. No one comes to the Father except through Me" (John 1:6).

Which message is the only one which makes sense. For there can only be two ways for sinners to be accepted by God: either do-it-yourself or receive-it-as-gift! And no one can do-it-yourself! Because God, as the Holy One, the One separate from sin, requires perfection: no sinning at all; and if there is sin, that sin must be paid for! Which Luther's "95 Theses" said can't be done! Can't buy forgiveness! We can't! Our "balloon" of innocence has been "popped" by the pin prick of even one sin, let alone the multitude of sins each of us is guilty of so that – like Humpty Dumpty – we can't be "put back together again". Do-it-yourself is impossible, no matter how many people attempt it in whatever form they use (all the different religions). So there is no hope for sinners, for us, in any do-it-yourself effort.

So Jesus said: "I am the way...no one comes...except through Me". Jesus is the only hope for sinners, for He has paid for our sin, "not with perishable things such as silver or gold...but with the precious blood of Christ" (1 Peter 1:18-19). Jesus was the sacrifice, the payment for sin, so that eternal life with God is "the gift of God" (Romans 6:23), "the gift of God – not by works, so that no one can boast" (Ephesians 2:8-9). That is the only way for anyone.

But that is not what many churches, even Lutheran churches, are now teaching. Instead, they teach that the Muslim god, Allah, is the same as the Christian God, the Triune God – just different names. And so faithful Muslims will be accepted by god-by-any-name not because of Jesus, but because they are faithful to their "god" (do-it-yourself, you see). And if Jesus paid for all, some say, then God must somehow accept all. Such is being taught more and more in so-called "Christian" churches.

And even worse! "God by another name"? How about a congregation, apparently in good standing with a Lutheran denomination in our country, which calls God "Sophia", "Womb", "Mother", "Goddess"? And its version of the Lord's Prayer begins: "Our Mother, who is within us, we celebrate your many names, your wisdom come, your will be done unfolding from the depths within us" – and the remainder is just as blasphemous (if you want to see this for yourself go to www.herchurch.org). Yet it is accepted as "Lutheran"? Of course, that same denomination not only approves of homosexuality, but even brags about electing practicing homosexuals to leadership positions – as do some other so-called "Christian" churches! Do we need another

Reformation? Absolutely!

And that Reformation has to begin at the same place it began for Luther and for King Josiah: the written Word of God, accepted as it is written, as God's truth with no "interpreting" it as containing "myths" or lacking "modern understandings of reality"! Instead: "It is written!" Good enough for Luther 500 years ago – good enough for King Josiah about 2700 years ago – has to be good enough for us no matter how "modern" we are! Because only as we accept this revelation of God will we receive God's true message of forgiveness of sins and eternal life through Jesus and only through Him.

But what can we as individuals do now to bring about a modern Reformation? Many people leave such Bible-denying churches (one denomination lost over half a million members in the last three years). A person can protest if Bible-denying ideas are taught in one's congregation. But one also needs to encourage one's pastor who is teaching faithfully, because pastors have to withstand much pressure from other clergy and even from misguided members to "not be so strict" regarding doctrine or godly living. Above all, we each need to be on guard lest we ourselves be misled in believing or in living according to our own desires to be accepted or to do what pleases our sinful natures instead of being faithful to what God's Word actually says. Which means that we need to be continually re-forming ourselves so that we admit the wrong we do, value the forgiveness we have because of Jesus, and ask His help to believe and live faithfully.

It is not likely that we will witness an historical reformation as happened because of Luther and because of King Josiah. But we can work on the basis of God's written Word so the congregation we belong to will be faithful and that we will be also.

October 27, 2013

Theme: **Thanksgiving Day**

Related Reading: Luke 7:11-19

Text: 1 Chronicles 16:34-36

THANKS FOR YOUR HELP

Undoubtedly the most followed American tradition at Thanksgiving is to eat turkey for the main meal (and often for meal after meal after that!). Another tradition followed by many is to watch a football game or a Thanksgiving Day parade. And other traditions which families follow at Thanksgiving time perhaps are: always gathering with relatives or making shopping plans for "black Friday". Family traditions are good to have.

A spiritual tradition which some families have is to go around the Thanksgiving table before beginning that turkey meal with each one telling what he or she is most thankful for from the past year. Probably most often this has to do with what things a person received or how well certain matters turned out in one's life or for the entire family. And so the typical prayer might begin: "Thank You, Lord, for..." It is good to be specific.

But perhaps a better form for that "thank You" prayer would be: "Thanks for Your help, Lord...", especially when a person is thanking Him for a personal accomplishment or a family blessing. We never receive or accomplish anything without His help and our effort. Yes, we have to make the effort! When we are sick, we have to take the prescribed medicine – but the Lord is the One Who helps by making that medicine effective and health-giving; when one needs a job, the job-hunter needs to send out the resumes and go to the interviews and perhaps even up-grade his or her skills, one cannot just sit at home and wait – but it is only by the Lord's help that conditions and employer needs meet together for a job to be offered; winning a sports championship requires much practice effort, but the Lord provides His help in keeping one healthy to compete; in any situation of need, we have to do our part, make our effort, but it is the Lord Who helps to work out the blessing. We call this His "mercy". So it is wise for us to pray: "Thanks for Your help, Lord!"

Such was the attitude of King David and the Israelites in our text, as they looked back at what the Lord had done in previous generations and as they considered their current somewhat precarious situation. They had had to fight, but the Lord had provided; now they still needed His help as they faced the future. So David told them to pray: "Cry out, 'Save us, O God our Savior; gather us and deliver us from the nations that we may give thanks to Your holy name, that we may glory in Your praise.'" That's how they were to pray – with the confidence that the Lord would help them so that David could also tell them: We can already thank Him, because we know He will help us even as He has in our past history: "Give thanks to the Lord, for He is good; His love endures forever...Praise be to the Lord, the God of Israel, from everlasting to everlasting." Thanks for Your help,

Lord, in what You have done in our past and in what You will do in our future! (By the way, David's words before our text were expanded to review the Lord's historical help in detail, which expansion became Psalm 105.)

This is how we also are to thank God even daily, but especially on a special day of thanks, such as Thanksgiving Day: Thanks for Your help in the past, Lord. And thank You even already for how You will help in the future. We are confident of Your help, Lord, we truly are! We will have to do our part – we have to make the effort – we also have to follow Your guidance so that we don't try to "cut corners" by doing what is not right or not quite right, but which seems more effective to us; but we confess and know that You have to provide the help we need, Lord, for life situations and desires and even dreams to turn out as blessings. So, thank You in advance, Lord, for Your help!

Actually, our confidence is based on more than our remembering how He has helped already in our lives and on even more than His promise to help us. Our confidence is based most of all on when He didn't help us at all! It is based on when He didn't "help" us, but did it *all* – without our effort. That was when He acted as our Savior, our Rescuer. For we were drowning in our sinning, and we could do nothing at all to rescue ourselves – He had to do it all – and He did!

Think of how a lifeguard rescues a person in danger of drowning. I remember from a swimming class probably 60 years ago when we were taught the side stroke. The instructor said, as I recall it, that this was the stroke one had to use when a person was in panic over imminent drowning. The rescuer had to get behind the person, grab him or her by the chin and side-stroke swim to safety. The panicked person couldn't help at all and could even make the danger worse to the point of drowning the rescuer also by flailing around wildly. But on his back with the rescuer pulling by the chin, rescue could be effected: not just the rescuer helping, but providing the complete rescue.

So did our Savior act as our Rescuer! No help from us – He did it all! Our efforts make our spiritual situation worse, when we claim to be good enough or if we despair that we are too bad to be cared about by God. Neither self-righteous pride nor guilty despair help in our rescue. Jesus had to do it all! Which He did by diving into our ocean of sin to live and die here, then reaching out through His message of forgiveness to pull us into the safety of faith for eternal life. Oh, we think we had to do our part; after all, we had to listen and then believe it. But His Word teaches that it was the Holy Spirit Who actually turned us from fighting against God's love in Christ – for that's what self-righteousness and despair are – into trusting acceptance of His work of rescuing us. Again, He did it all – we only benefit.

And because He did so rescue us, we trust His help as we live now. He has helped us through difficult times in the past – He will continue to so help us. He has provided for us in the past – He will continue to do so.

Which is why not only in a special Thanksgiving way but every day, we will pray: *Thanks for Your help, Lord, in the past and how You will help in the future.*

November 24, 2013

Theme: **End of This Life**

Related Reading: 1 Thessalonians 4:13-18

Text: Job 19:25-27

LIFE! IN BETWEEN! AND ALSO!

And so, sooner or later we are going to die – unless Judgment Day comes first! And although we know, well, we believe – for no one can absolutely prove it, so: although we believe that after this life will be far better for us than the best of this life, unless we are in the midst of an absolutely miserable time of life, it is natural that we hope death comes later rather than sooner. Why? Because this life is what we know, and we can't imagine not existing in this life. At least I think that most of us feel that way. And the closer we come to the inevitable, the more likely we feel this way.

No, we don't truly "know" about life after death. True, many people have experienced what is called "life after life", a "near death" experience in which a person, who has been declared "dead", is told by an angelic-appearing being: Not your time yet. I have known a number of individuals who experienced this – and very likely St. Paul did also according to 2 Corinthians 12. In contrast are those various people – including very recently a child – who claim to have actually been to heaven and back. But when one examines their claims, one sees either impossible experiences (such as: Jesus personally taking the person in His arms and onto His lap upon arrival – how could He do that for each person when probably hundreds of Christians die every minute?) or claims which conflict with what Scripture teaches (such as, unborn "souls" waiting to be born). No, we can't believe anyone who claims to have been to heaven and back.

Still, we believe we will live after we die, for Scripture says so – the whole book of Revelation teaches this. And why else did Jesus come and obey and suffer and die except to be "the way" to "come to the Father" (John 14:68)? So, we believe we will have life in heaven after this life.

However, do we all realize or keep in mind that life in "heaven" will be only for a while? Not forever? No, because Scripture clearly teaches, both by the fact of Jesus' bodily resurrection and by clear statements of Jesus (such as in Matthew 22: "at the resurrection", v.30) that after "heaven", being in God's presence without a physical body, we will finally experience a re-creation of our bodies for eternal life in God's new creation (as He promises us in 1 Corinthians 15 and 2 Peter 3 among other places as well as the claim of Job in our text – and the "peaceable kingdom" of Isaiah 11, which we will think about in next week's "Message").

So, we believe according to Scripture that after we die, we will continue to live without our bodies and without any connection to this life in God's very presence – until the end of this world, when God will cause "the resurrection of the body" with "the life everlasting" after that (as we confess in the Apostles' Creed – the Nicene Creed stating the same with slightly different wording: "the resurrection of the dead and the life of the world to come") – that is what awaits us.

Which is what Job believed already in the Old Testament: "after my skin has been destroyed, yet in my flesh I will see God; I myself will see Him with my own eyes – I, and not another". He knew he would die – he knew his body would decay – yet, because of His "Redeemer", he would get his body back to see the Lord "in the end" when "He will stand upon the earth".

Hmm, but Job says nothing about the in-between, the time between death and that final re-creation day. Which may be partly why some, who claim to be teaching according to Scripture, claim that those who have died actually have no consciousness during that time, but, instead, truly "sleep", for doesn't even Paul write about the dead as "those who have fallen asleep in Him (Jesus)" (1 Thessalonians 4:14)? However, Paul is using this picture of death as sleep so that we don't fear death any more than we fear falling asleep. But Jesus says clearly that the dead are alive. He told the Sadducees (Matthew 22:32): "I am the God of Abraham, the God of Isaac, and the God of Jacob – He is not God of the dead but of the living". Not "asleep", but alive! Doing what? Can't say for sure according to what Scripture says other than we will be "praising" the Lord .

However, does that mean we will only be singing in a mass heavenly choir all the time? Not necessarily, since "praise" is not merely verbal words to God; praise also is "the fruit of lips that confess His name" (Hebrews 13:15), which takes place also when we speak to each other about what the Lord has done for us in our lives as well as eternally. So it seems reasonable to assume that we will talk with our fellow children of God who have entered heaven through death, including also our loved ones in Christ and perhaps even the great heroes of faith, for it would be praise of the Lord by them to tell us of how He worked in their lives on earth. However, we can't know for sure exactly what life in the Lord's eternal presence will involve. We only know for sure that it will be good, a joy for us.

Of course, more important than what we will do there is getting there! So, why was Job confidently believing that, although he would die and his body would decay, he would live and receive a re-created body? Very boldly Job confessed his faith: "I know that my Redeemer lives". Job was one of the most faithful children of God who ever lived according to what God Himself said: "There is no one on earth like him; he is blameless and upright, a man who fears God and shuns evil" (1:8). Job really obeyed – as much as humanly possible! Still, Job knew he wasn't good enough – he still needed a "Redeemer", One Who would "redeem" him, pay the necessary price to set him free before God from his sins against God. Job is not only a great example of trust in God even when suffering severely – he also is a great example of humility before God: I've tried, Lord, but I'm not good enough – I need One to redeem me, to set me free from the consequences of my sinning.

If Job needed that faith, do we need it any less? For can

any of us claim to be a great example of faithfulness? True, we have tried – and to a certain extent succeeded, although only by the Lord's power working in us; but never so well that we could claim praise for our efforts – always we must confess: Lord, be merciful to me, a sinner. For that's what we always are, each of us, a sinner, and often our sinning shows itself in a bit of pride: but not really too bad, Lord! Oh? The Lord pays no attention to "not as bad as" or even "at least I tried" – He sees only: sinner! Who needs a Redeemer!

And the Lord said this already before creation (which is beyond our understanding): you, as well as Job, as well as everyone else, you need a Redeemer. So did He judge us! But then He also made His plan to redeem us through His Son, come to earth as the "Redeemer", paying to rescue us by not only His suffering and death, but also by His perfect obeying. Jesus has redeemed us! He has paid the price required for us sinners!

Which is our comfort and confidence and joy! We trust this message from God, given to us through Job in this text as well as through the other writers of Scripture, in the Old Testament which pointed ahead to Him, in the New Testament which points back to His completion of God's plan, the redemption Jesus accomplished. We trust this is so! And we also with Job claim "my Redeemer", Jesus!

Not one of us knows when the Lord will say to us: Now is your time to come to Me! But it does not really matter. We are trusting His Word for where we are finally going because of Jesus. And He is why we will try to be like Job in living as faithfully as possible whatever comes in life here until we enter life there.

November 10, 2013

Theme: **Life Everlasting**
Related Reading: 2 Peter 3:3-14
Text: Isaiah 11:1-9

THE PEACEABLE KINGDOM

The last three doctrines which we confess in the Apostles' Creed are: "the forgiveness of sins, the resurrection of the body, and the life everlasting". Those three teachings are prophesied by Isaiah in the three paragraphs of our text.

"A shoot will come up from the stump of Jesse" foretells the coming of Jesus into the world with the remainder of the paragraph outlining His perfect life so He could be the sacrifice to pay for "the forgiveness of sins" for all sinners.

The second paragraph speaks of His being the judge of the world, which will take place on Judgment Day, which also will be the day of "the resurrection of the body" for all who have died, although with the difference, of course, that those who actually trust in Jesus – which had shown in their lives of helping people in need – will rise for eternal life with and for God, while those who rejected or only pretended to accept this faith will face eternal existence and condemnation apart from God.

The third paragraph then describes "the life everlasting" in terms that have long been called "The Peaceable Kingdom" in which "the wolf will live with the lamb" without violence, "the cow will feed with the bear...and the lion will eat straw like the ox" – no meat-eating by any animal, and a child "will play near the hole of the cobra" and even be able to "put his hand into the viper's nest" without danger, because "they will neither harm nor destroy on all My holy mountain". And then that glorious promise: "the earth will be full of the knowledge of the Lord as the waters cover the seas". Truly, "the life everlasting" will be the peaceable kingdom for us!

There is much that could be explained in each of these three prophecies, but this "Message" will concentrate mostly on "The Peaceable Kingdom", while briefly explaining the first two. So: we know about and trust in what Jesus did in His time of human existence on earth, that He had to come if anyone would ever be able to experience this peaceable kingdom, because selfishness leading eventually to violence, if one doesn't get his or her own way, is the record of our lives. "That's mine" says a current Cadillac ad, as the older brother keeps taking things away from the younger one – until the younger one is successful enough to own a Cadillac and say: "That's mine" to his older brother and drive away in revenge. And actual living gets worse including spousal and child abuse, criminal acts, governmental confiscation, war – while violence is also the mark of animals: kill or be killed. Jesus didn't suffer and die for animals, but He did as the innocent sacrifice for us sinning humans. Jesus as Savior!

But also Jesus is Judge! On that last day of this creation "He will come to judge the living and the dead", as we also confess in the Creed. The striking thing about the judging, however, is not that He will ask: Did you have faith in Me as Savior? Instead, since mere words don't amount to "a hill of beans", as the saying goes, He will declare: "Come, you who are blessed by My Father, take your inheritance, the kingdom prepared for you since the creation of the world" (Matthew 25:34). This was God's plan all along: to have people live in and enjoy His kingdom, His "peaceable kingdom". He made it possible for those who had become His enemies by their sinning, made it possible through Jesus, to become His children, who would receive this "inheritance" as a given not a reward, a present not a payment. No way sinners could ever pay – so Jesus did. And the Holy Spirit worked trust in Jesus in them to make them His blessed children: we are "the children of God through faith in Christ Jesus" (Galatians 3:26). Yet this faith is not merely words nor is it an un-lose-able gift to us by Baptism or by a personal confession of faith (followed by God's stamp of adoption in Baptism). Faith always will show, show by helping the actual needy – so Jesus the Judge will say in His judgment sentence: "I was hungry and you fed Me" and so on according to Matthew, while unbelievers are those who refused to help and made excuses instead.

Which brings us soberly to repentance! For we don't always help as we could and should! Selfishness is still a part of us and too easily motivates us. Which humbles us always into: Lord, be merciful to me, a sinner! Which is why on that Judgment Day we will not remember the helping we did, since the holiness of God will be reminding us instead of how unworthy we are because of our failures. So, "with righteousness He will judge the needy" (us), the spiritually needy, giving His righteousness to us sinners who trust not in ourselves or any of our deeds, but only in His perfect, righteous sacrifice.

And then will come "the peaceable kingdom", the new creation, the creation God originally intended, but which a rebellious angel corrupted by injecting disobedience, sin, into the first humans. But now there will never be sin or its consequences, for "the knowledge of the Lord" will fill us forgiven sinners, knowledge not merely of what He commands, but mostly of how He loves us, so that we will love, that is, serve Him perfectly.

Which will be a joyful delight, not a grudging duty, as so often it is in us now because of our sinful nature. No violence in any degree at all, not by human nor by animal, but peace – and enjoyment of one another, for, if the children will enjoy the animals, won't we all also enjoy each other?

Brings up the question of age! Apparently there will be "the little child", "the infant", "the young child", because Isaiah's prophecy says so. Is that the age when they died? So, will we be the visible age in the peaceable kingdom as when we died? Can't really say for sure, although it sounds reasonable – with the provision that the body we have here will be changed in that (says Paul in 1 Corinthians 15) it will be "imperishable", even have "immortality" and have "power" (vs.42-43,53-54). By the way, Paul calls this "changed" body a "spiritual body", but that does not mean "ghost-like" as strictly "spirit". Can't be, because Jesus was not "a ghost", as the disciples first thought and reacted. Instead, Jesus showed He still had His "flesh and bones" (Luke 24:36-39), and "we shall be like Him" (1 John 3:2), because our resurrection will be like His!

Actually, we can't get too definite about details of life in the peaceable kingdom. We can imagine on the basis of what God has revealed in Scripture (and Isaiah 35 is another beautiful description), but always with the disclaimer: it could be, but really we'll just have to wait and see.

But we can be sure: peace – between animals, between animals and humans, between us who will be there, not because we deserve it, but strictly because of Jesus, our Savior. And the knowing of that peace and blessedness eventually being ours because of Him helps us not only to endure life now in our selfish, violence-prone world with all the aches and pains, emotional as well as physical, which we must now endure, but also to work as well as we can to make this life more enjoyable and peaceable, wherever we live.

November 17, 2013

CHRISTIAN FAITH
and
LIVING

Theme: **Our God**

Related Reading: Philippians 2:1-11

Text: Exodus 3:12-15

THE GREAT I AM

It's almost becoming a custom in our country when something horrific happens in a community that all the churches come together for a joint prayer service to express sympathy and outrage and to comfort those whose loved ones have died. There was 9/11, the New Town school massacre, after some tornado devastations to name a few. Nothing wrong with that, is there? A good thing, right?

Well, one could say that such services had real value and comfort if all the churches involved were truly Christian to speak with one voice. However, the qualifying word there is "truly" Christian, because not all churches who claim to be "Christian" actually are. Some teach some doctrines which clearly contradict what Scripture definitely teaches, so one has to be careful when the name "Christian" is used. On the other hand, when those services involve many different religions, not just different Christian denominations but different religions, which believe in different "gods", such services are an abomination! Not my judgment – God's condemnation!

But, preacher! There's only one god, isn't there, and all are praying to that one god, even though they use different names, aren't they?

Hardly! For people do worship different "gods" and define their "god" in specific ways so that, for example, the Muslim "god", whom they call "Allah", has no similarity to the true God, Who is revealed in Scripture. Allah is a cruel, vindictive god, who demands obedience, submission, without mercy! Steal and have your hand cut off! Be caught in adultery and be stoned to death (of course, usually only the woman gets that punishment)! Say something disrespectful of Allah and have your head cut off! Mercy, forgiveness? Not from Allah!

What a contrast to the true God, the "I am Who I am" of Scripture and specifically in our text! The God of mercy – helping people; the God of grace – forgiving people, because He took out His anger against sin upon His own Son, actually upon Himself, since God the Son is fully God as well as being a Person of God! No way the God Who is "I am" can be "the same" as Allah!

Or the Hindu "god" – well, "gods", since various animals are considered "god" as well as the ultimate "light", which has no personality at all. And again, no mercy, no forgiveness, only obedience according to the law of karma. Please! Do not insult the true God, the "I am Who I am", by comparing Him to any Hindu god! Same regarding any other organized religion including Wiccaism and even Judaism. For although "I am Who I am" was the God of Israel, their religious beliefs have turned away from Him to their own idea of "god", who is only "one" and who has no grace for sinners available through Jesus by His life and

146

death. No! You have to be a Jew to receive blessing from their "god"! The fact is that people do believe in different "gods", not merely in different names!

And the true God, the "I am Who I am", will tolerate no other god! The first commandment He gave to the Israelites, whom He had chosen to be His people so He could send His Son into human existence in order to save sinning humans, His first commandment was – and remains: "You shall have no other gods before Me" (which can be translated "beside Me" or even "in My Presence")! No other gods! None! He claims to be the only God! He neither recognizes nor allows any other god as existing! No other gods! Only Him! Which means that to try to give equal status or even any status at all to other gods is an abomination! And also means that any human being who claims other gods are merely other names does not know or trust in or follow the true God at all!

Which brings up a related question about God: does God actually exist? More and more people even in our country believe He doesn't! And even more people live their lives as though no god exists! That is the whole purpose behind the belief in evolution: no god was needed to have life and all creatures come into existence – and none is needed since then! Actually, if you believe in evolution, the form technically called "macro-evolution" – from nothing to chemical to life to all living forms as well as the development of the universe itself – if you believe that, then you are also believing in atheism, you are approving of the

147

belief that there is no God nor any other god. Nor can you weasel your way out by claiming that God "used" evolution to "create" life and everything else. For the macro-evolution process denies the existence of any god form at all. So you face not a "both-and" but an "either-or"!

Still, we who believe that God does exist do believe also that God has worked changes in the various forms of life – it's called "micro-evolution", so that God created one man and one woman from whom all the varieties of human beings descended with the shuffling of chromosomes causing all our human varieties. Same for every life form: one cat pair developed into lions and tigers and house cats, etc. – again, to over-simplify: the shuffling of chromosomes producing those changes. But no crossover from one distinct "form" (called "kind" in Genesis 1) to another: micro-evolution/change, yes; macro-evolution/chemical-to-human, absolutely not!

But the question again: does God truly exist or not? Is the evolution belief perhaps correct that God doesn't? Frankly, there is no proof, no absolute proof, for either option! Shocking? But true! For each is a "belief", and a "belief" is just that: an unprovable assumption – although that assumption is based on evidence. Note: 2 + 2 = 4 is not a belief – that is a fact, just as you do not "believe" you have a physical body – you have one as a fact. But a "belief" is being convinced about something without being able to factually prove it.

And so evolutionists "believe" there is no God or god, because they claim there is no evidence and everything in their evolution belief "works" without the need for God/god. To which we answer: but how did anything get here in the very first place? If there was nothing to begin with, how could "no thing" produce "some thing"? No! As God's Word says in Hebrews (3:4): "Every house is built by someone, but God is the builder of everything". Just plain common sense says that Someone has to be behind everything! And when we see how intricately even just our blood is made with all its components and our bodies in all its parts, can any unbiased thinking person truly judge: by chance? Those who do, do so because they don't want anyone to condemn them for their evil thinking and evil doing – that's what's truly the bias behind the evolutionistic belief. As God's Word also says (Psalm 14:1): "The fool says in his heart, 'There is no God'" – and why? "They are corrupt, their deeds are vile", which means: no god to tell me what to do or not to do – most of which is connected to sex and greed. We believe in God's existence with good reason – the existence of the universe. But the atheists have no good reason for their belief – they only want to be free to be as immoral and as greedy for things and power as they can be.

Also, our specific belief is not in just a general "god" or "being" or "force", but in the very personal God Who is and Who has acted with mercy and grace for us. For we all know we are guilty before God, yes, of sexual sinning and of greed as well as all our other types of sinning. Yet His constant "Gospel", good news, is that He has acted so He can and does forgive us. He did this in Jesus, come into this physical world to have a physical body to live a human life. He lived it – perfectly! With no sinning! So that He could take all of our sinning onto Himself in order to nullify it in God's judgment process so that God, the "I am Who I am", can judge us: innocent! and can welcome us into His Presence without fear to be blessed forever. This is why we believe, trust, the only true, the only existing God: because of His action to save us through Jesus.

All of which means for us, first, that we do not have to ever be ashamed of our belief in Him, our faith – those who oppose us with their beliefs have far less evidence for their belief than we have for ours. It's all "belief", either way!

Next, we need to be faithful to God, not insult Him by giving any recognition to other "gods" – which means that we dare not participate in inter-religion prayer services. We should give human sympathy to those who have suffered loss – we should also give physical help, if we are able to. But we cannot comfort anyone spiritually who does not trust in Jesus as Savior. For there is no comfort in any tragedy – or at any death – except through faith in Jesus.

But as we help those who are hurting and suffering, we may be able to speak God's good news about Jesus. Yet, even if that opportunity doesn't arise, we truly serve our God, the great I am, when we help others endure and recover from whatever tragedy or trouble they are facing.

And we sure have many opportunities to do that in our sinful, violence-prone world.

April 14, 2013

Theme: **Grace**

Related Reading: Ephesians 2:1-10

Text: Romans 5:18-21

ENOUGH GRACE, EVEN FOR YOU

The theme of this "Message" is God's grace, His undeserved love for us sinners which results in the forgiveness of sins. But what can I possibly share with you that you don't know already? However, a preacher's responsibility is not to tell you something new, but to help you think through again what is true in an interesting way (so you truly think it through) and how that relates to our daily living. Which I will try to do on the basis of this text from Romans.

When I looked at this text early in the week, an old saying came to my mind: "One for all and all for one" – which happens to be the traditional motto of the cantons of Switzerland and also was the motto in Alexandre Dumas' book, "The Three Musketeers". The saying itself, however, was first prominently used in 1618 by the Protestant leaders in Prague as a summary of their defense pact against the Roman Catholic kings who were trying to force them and their lands back into submission to the pope – this precipitated the Thirty Years War between Protestant and Roman Catholic countries.

In thinking of this motto for our text, it was not in a defense pact sense, however. Instead, it was simply a different way of understanding what God's grace did. Once sin entered God's creation through the "one trespass" of Adam (and Eve, of course), condemnation came upon every human being to ever be born (except one, Jesus, of course). How can that be? How can that sin in the Garden of Eden condemn even you and me? Because that one sin contaminated the human race. And even though it would now be, one could say, diluted to only one part in so many billions of human actions since then, still the contamination never is eliminated by human activity – and God's justice says that any contamination is fatal, is unacceptable, produces condemnation. We want to argue that this is not fair. But the fact is that that contamination is what produces all of our actual sinning: everyone is contaminated by Adam's sin, and so everyone sins. All this sin contamination has continued ever since Adam.

So, God's grace, His undeserved love, led Him to act against all that contamination. He acted, as we know, by having part of Himself (to use human terminology to describe what we really cannot understand) become human in the Person of Jesus, God come to earth, that is, receiving human nature into His divine nature in order to truly live here in time as one of us human beings. And all the sins of every other human being became His responsibility so that we can say: "all for One".

So, as the one initial sin by Adam contaminated everyone and all that condemnation was given to the One Person, Jesus Christ, God with us, "so also the result of one act of righteousness was justification that brings life for all men (and women)...through the obedience of the One Man the many will be made righteous" so that we can say: "One for all" – all that Jesus did by His one act of obedient righteousness, that is, as Paul explains in Philippians: "being found in appearance as a man, He humbled Himself and became obedient to death – even death on a cross" (2:8): "One for all".

A couple of related questions: first, how could one take responsibility for all? Only because He was not merely a man, human, but because He was God, actually and fully God – only in that reality could He be "big enough" to be "enough" for "all". If Jesus was only a man, as some "pretend" Christians teach, he could not have even helped himself escape the condemnation of sin, for he would also have been contaminated and would also have given in to temptation and needed rescue. But He was God as well as man – that is how He could be the "One for all".

Another question, a double one: the text says that His act of righteousness (suffering unto death on the cross) "brings life for all men (and women)", yet then the text goes on to say that "through the obedience of the One Man the many will be made righteous" – sounds almost like a contradiction ("all" vs. "the many"). One perhaps could resolve this by saying that the Greek words for "the many" actually meant everyone, at least, all the ordinary people, the common people. But that doesn't actually resolve it, because the upper class people would then be left out (they were not

154

considered part of the *"hoi poloi"*, the many). The answer actually is: Jesus' one act of righteousness, of obedience unto death, made it possible for all sinners to receive this life which goes on for all eternity. However, only some will actually benefit, "will be made righteous", because this life is received only "through faith": only those who actually depend only on what Jesus did to deliver them from their sins, from even the contamination stretching back to Adam, only those actually receive what Jesus made possible. This is called "justification (being declared righteous and, therefore, being "made righteous" in God's judgment) by faith" – "for it is by grace you are saved, through faith" (Ephesians 2:8).

This is the "history" of God's grace in action toward us sinners. Theologically it is called "objective justification" (it has already been done for everyone) and "subjective justification" (it becomes your personal benefit when you come to faith in Jesus as Savior).

But we sinners by nature don't like this reality, because, we argue, one man's sin long ago shouldn't condemn me now – I can't be blamed for what he did! So, as our text goes on, God acted: "The law was added so that the trespass might increase" – the law of God, as summarized in the Ten Commandments, confronts us to make us realize it isn't just the contamination by Adam's sin – it is our sinning also! It is not as though there gets to be more sin because of God's law (although this also is true in that sometimes we humans do just the opposite of what we are told to do), but God's law makes us realize, makes us admit, that we have sinned and do sin, so we are guilty and need forgiveness. If a sinner never admits his/her eternal need, that sinner will have no interest in Someone to take care of that need. But when I know I need it, I am thankful to receive it, to have that "eternal life through Jesus Christ, our Lord".

Except sometimes in guilt I might doubt that God's grace actually can include me – after what I've done! This is particularly how this "Message" about God's grace is to benefit you and me in our daily living. Most of the time we are just thankful for His grace – and we live in a sense of peace, because we know we truly are forgiven, which shows itself in how we try to live His way. But every once in a while guilt can almost overwhelm us – and for some people guilt is a constant overwhelming burden. Maybe it has never happened to you personally – but it might about some particular sinning, even if it was not an evil deed, truly evil and impossible for a Christian to do (see Galatians 5:19-21 and Ephesians 5:3-6); yet it comes back at you: "how could I?" and "can God really accept me, especially when I've done it again?" Then you and I must remind ourselves: Jesus was the "One for all" so there is enough grace, even for me! Which is God's special assurance in Holy Communion – or when a pastor or a fellow Christian tells us: yes, your sins are forgiven! Because of what Jesus did for us all, there is enough grace even for you!

But this fact – or shall we say this "motto" of: Enough Grace, Even for You, is the absolute assurance a guilt-stricken person needs – whether you because of some evil in your past life or a friend of yours, who does have a past evil which keeps him or her in doubt or perhaps a person you have come to know who is presently living in evil – not liking it and wanting to escape it, but with that condemning thought: God surely can't accept me! Perhaps it is a woman who had an abortion and now grieves – or the man who made her get that abortion! Perhaps it is a sexual affair which one had been in, but still feels guilt about. Perhaps it is a veteran, who still is plagued with guilt over what he or she had to do in combat. Perhaps it is some meanness you are guilty of toward a helpless individual long ago. Perhaps it is an alcoholic who "fell off the wagon" – again! Perhaps a drug addict who is struggling to quit, but doesn't seem able to – perhaps it is just something you are now still ashamed of having done to someone, not necessarily truly evil, but you still feel bad because you know it wasn't right or you wanted to hurt. Guilt can attack us over so much from our past – with the thought: No, God can't truly accept me!

When such times come, especially then we remember: Jesus did do enough – He was the One – Who came – for all – all people – all sins. All were loaded upon Him: all for One; and He truly is the One for all: all sins, all sinners, which means, yes, even for you! So, relax in His peace – relax in peace so that you can this day live thankfully His way – as His new, His justified, creation.

February 9, 2014

Theme: **Word of God**

Related Reading: 2 Timothy 3:10-17

Text: Luke 8:4-15

HOW IS YOUR GARDEN GROWING?

Given how many people like to "play" with plants and dirt, whether farming, gardening, landscaping, or tending house plants, one might wonder if God has put a gardening instinct into us, just as He has created us with the paternal/maternal instinct. One might even wonder whether those acting on this gardening instinct (it that's what it is) could possibly be practicing for work in the new creation, after all, in the original creation man's responsibility was "to work (the Garden of Eden) and care for it" (Genesis 2:15); and in the new, eternal, creation we will not merely stand around to sing praises, but will have work to do. However, the details of that work we'll just have to wait to see.

Jesus in His preaching and teaching often used illustrations, which is what parables are, illustrations to help explain a teaching truth; usually He based His illustrations on the agricultural life-style, which all of His hearers were well-acquainted with. So in our text Jesus uses the example of the farmer scattering his seed, which is how they planted the fields at that time and the ground being farmed. With this parable Jesus also gives a quite-detailed, although not quite complete, explanation. By the way, this parable is quoted almost identically in Matthew (13:1-23) and Mark (4:1-20), the differences being due apparently to Jesus having used it on different occasions – in His three-year public ministry Jesus was not above repeating Himself at times.

Jesus' basic explanation is: "the seed is the Word of God", the soil conditions – hardpan, rocky, thorn-infested, and good – refer to how people hear that message from God: automatic rejection, only if it's easy, as long as it doesn't interfere with what they want to do, or letting it achieve its intended purpose: producing a crop – which for God's people would be: the daily deeds of kindness, goodness, helping, since those are the works, the fruit, the "crop" which God always expects and produces as the outcome of faith according to Ephesians 2:10 and Romans 12 as well as other passages.

Some clarifications: first, although the *result* of the power of God's message, when it does its work, is to cause faith to begin so we have forgiveness of our sins, the *purpose* of the power of God's message is that the forgiven sinner will show in daily living that he/she *is* a forgiven child of God (Ephesians 2:10 again). It's exactly the same as growing a plant: the plant always has a *purpose* – not merely to exist, but to provide food or beauty or – in the case of thorns and thistles – to be a reminder of Adam's fall into sin so that no place on earth can ever be an absolute "paradise" (Genesis 3:17-19). So our purpose when we have come to faith for forgiveness, is "to live a life worthy of the calling (we) have received" (Ephesians 4:1), since "faith without deeds is dead" (James 2:26). The production quantity may vary, as Jesus says in our text; but the quality will always be evident, the quality of doing what God says because of what God did for us in Jesus.

Second clarification: the "plant" of faith is not something that we decide on, whether to believe, to trust Jesus, or not. It feels that way at initial contact, of course. But where does a plant come from? From the soil or from the seed? The fact is that soil conditions can kill the seed and what it produces, but it is the power of that seed which produces the plant itself. Exactly the same spiritually: we through our sinful nature have the power to prevent faith and also to kill it. But we don't have the power to produce faith – or even to keep it growing! The seed, the Word of God, specifically the message about what Jesus has done to rescue us from our sins, that is what creates faith in a person, as Paul wrote in Romans 10: "faith comes from hearing the message" (v.17). True, we have to decide to hear that message and then to pay attention to understand it, for faith does not come out in the middle of nowhere with no words being spoken or heard. To be sure, we can be impressed by the power of God through the magnificence of His created works, but that is not faith in Jesus as Savior. Merely believing God exists does not give anyone forgiveness of sins. Forgiveness is ours only as we trust in Jesus as the only One Who could and did do everything required to spare us from the consequences of our sinning. And even though we physically have to get into contact with those words, it is the power of the words, the message of Jesus, which causes faith to begin and grow. Again from agriculture: the ground does not produce the plant – the seed is the power. We can reject that power, but we are not able to even decide to let that power work – the power of the Word of God about Jesus does it all.

However, once that power, that seed, that Word of God, that message of Jesus, has entered our brains, then what happens, what do we do with that message? This is really the point Jesus is making through this parable. Will we just automatically reject what God is trying to tell us? Happens easily – perhaps even often – also among us who have come to faith in Jesus. Just because someone is physically hearing something, doesn't mean he or she is paying any attention. And don't you have to confess, as I do, that after having heard (or for us right now: read) a message of God's Word, so easily we can forget what the message was about and so fail to "retain it", as Jesus says in our text, to let it influence our attitudes or actions? Sometimes I will read a daily devotion at breakfast, only to have to admit to not even remembering what it was about by mid-morning! Also, sometimes we can be truly impressed by the message, be thankful for it at the time, but then reject it by silence (at least for a while) when challenged by someone who doesn't believe. And then when we have to make a choice between faithful godly living and "worries, riches, pleasures", as Jesus mentioned, how often don't we choose things of this life at the expense of faithfulness to our Savior? Bluntly, how are you responding to the Word of God? How is your garden, your spiritual garden, growing?

To grow a physical garden plant you need to neutralize poor soil conditions and then provide fertilizer and water. Spiritually, we neutralize the spiritual ground of our thinking by being on guard against our own attempts to ignore His message, which usually is caused by our pride which says: I don't need this, because I'm a pretty good person. To which God's Word says: No, you are not! Not good enough! Not really all that good even! So you need what Jesus has done! God's Word says: you need Him so much that you dare not ignore Him or fear others more than you trust in Him or choose temporary things over Him! You need Him! Our pride must be so "neutralized".

But physically neutralizing destructive soil conditions is only the first step in producing a crop. Once the seed is planted, fertilizer and water are needed, if a crop is to result. Spiritually speaking, Jesus is the "fertilizer" and the "water" our "plant" of faith needs regularly in order to produce its God-intended "crop". Jesus called Himself the "Bread of life" (John 6:35) and the "water" which satisfies and leads to eternal life (John 4:10-14). So He is the "fertilizer" (food) and "water" we need to stay alive spiritually and to be growing in crop production. Not that He has set a quota which we must fulfill to be accepted at last, for that would mean we would be entering eternal life because of what we do instead of because of what He did! But we are to keep on living His way and so growing His "crop".

How? The seed, the Word, His message, is the power to produce the plant of faith, agreed? And that same seed/Word/message is the power to keep our plant of faith alive and producing. Which means: we must faithfully use the Word! hear it (with our ears and/or our eyes)! keep it in mind as we live, that is, keep in mind that He has rescued us and given us spiritual life to live! and then let His power from His Word flow through us to do the deeds of good which we have opportunity to do as we live daily.

That's how our spiritual garden keeps growing!

September 9, 2012

Theme: **Baptism**

Related Reading: Romans 6:1-11

Text: Colossians 2:11-15

THEIR CIRCUMCISION – OUR BAPTISM

Although every proper "Message" (sermon) will include both instruction or explanation of Scriptural teaching for our faith and application of that teaching for our living, this week's "Message" has more emphasis on instruction than usual. For I have to explain more about the Old Testament sacrament of circumcision ("sacrament", because it did bring God's grace to a specific individual) so that we will better understand – and believe – the value of our New Testament sacrament of Baptism.

Some Christians do not use the term "sacrament". Instead they call both Baptism and Holy Communion "ordinances", commands of God to be obeyed. And it is true: both – as also the Old Testament circumcision and Passover – were commanded – in the sense that those who trust in Jesus as Savior are to receive them. But these are not "commands" which we "do" as our effort to obey; these are actions of God which we are to receive. That is, we do not "do" Baptism – God acts toward us; we do not "do" Holy Communion – God is giving to us Jesus' very Body and Blood; and Old Testament circumcision very obviously was done to the baby boy (or adult convert), who did nothing except perhaps cry. So, "ordinance" is not a suitable word for these specific ceremonies which God's people are to receive.

But to explain the parallel and the difference between their circumcision in the Old Testament and our Baptism in the New Testament: circumcision was God's physical and daily visible sign to each male of Israel that God had adopted him into His people on earth – anyone who refused to be circumcised was to be "cut off from His people" (Genesis 17:14), meaning, not to be accepted as one of God's people. (Why God had no special visible sign for females, God never explained; but since they were always part of an Israelite family, they saw the male visible sign to know they also were included.)

Being circumcised did not guarantee that that male would live with God forever, but only that God had adopted him and wanted him. The history of the Old Testament people showed already in the Exodus years and especially later, when they as a nation had settled in Palestine, that most of them ended up rejected by God, because, as Hebrews 4:2 says: "they did not combine it with faith".

Our Christian Baptism is parallel yet different in that it also is God's personal sign to an individual that He has adopted him or her (females are given the sign also) into His family. It is not an on-going physically visible sign, but a spiritual assurance: you have been washed free of your sins, not like dirt by water, but by the sacrificed blood of Jesus so that you can have a "good conscience" (meaning: a conscience at peace because you have been forgiven) in spite of your sinning (1 Peter 1:12-14, 3:21). Just like with circumcision Baptism is God's action, which the baby receives – it can't refuse – so "faith", trust in the action and promise of God, is begun at that time by the Holy Spirit. However, if faith is lost – whether neglected or rejected – as the child becomes an adult, the promised blessing is lost.

God's "good news" (Gospel) message always is: your sins have already been forgiven! When? When God, as our text specifically says, "forgave us all our sins, having canceled the written code with its regulations that was against us and that stood opposed to us; He took it away, nailing it to the cross". When Jesus suffered and died, He said at the last: "It is finished", meaning, the work of earning forgiveness is "finished", completed – the debt of sin has been completely paid!

That is always God's message to us: it has all been done! I have forgiven you all your sins already! Believe it! Trust that I have because of what Jesus did! In a sense God is even saying: Let Me do it! Don't argue that you have to do something to deserve forgiveness! I've done it – everything needed – through Jesus! Let Me do it My way, because there is no other way! Even as Jesus said: "I am the way...no one comes to the Father except through Me" (John 14:6).

This is the message especially of Baptism: you – whether a baby or an adult – you – and I know you by name – you are helpless before Me; but I have washed you clean of your sins – through Jesus – trust Me on this!

This is always the "good news": you have been forgiven already – trust this My promise to you! You don't have to do a thing! Jesus did it all! You don't even have to "invite Me into your heart and life" or "really" mean what you say or have to meet some minimum requirement of living! You just let Me forgive you – because of Jesus! That's the Scriptural message in preaching, in baptizing, in Holy Communion: it's all been done! Trust that Jesus has done it!

Of course, when we do so "let Him do it", trust what He says, then something changes in us, whether as a baby or as a hearing adult. And let's be clear that it can happen in a baby as well as in a knowing adult, because why does anyone trust God's promise of forgiveness through Jesus? It is not a "personal decision" after rationally weighing the pros and cons – although to an adult it feels that way; it is not a work on our part. Coming to faith is strictly because the Holy Spirit causes us somehow to believe, to trust, and to keep trusting. Our text says: "you were dead in your sins...God made you alive with Christ" – as also Paul wrote to the Corinthians: "no one can say: 'Jesus is Lord' except by the Holy Spirit" (I,12:3) – faith, trust, letting God do it – this is the Holy Spirit's doing: somehow He overcomes the pride and resistance of those who do come to trust His promise – humanly speaking, it's easier for Him to cause that trust to begin in a baby, because the baby hasn't learned any adult arguments yet. But at every age it is the working of the Holy Spirit that causes faith.

Of course – and this "of course" has to be explained

before the previous one about the change that takes place in us – of course, that trust is never a "one and done" experience – it has to continue. So the Holy Spirit works through our thinking process about the "I've done it all already" message. In the Old Testament whenever the male saw his circumcision, whenever the family celebrated the Passover, the message was: see what the Lord has done – trust His promise! Exactly the same for us in the New Testament! Whether we hear the promise preached or read it ourselves or think about Baptism or receive Holy Communion, the Holy Spirit is telling us: It's all been done – don't let your pride or the arguments of unbelievers get in the way – trust what He has done! He has forgiven you – because of Jesus!

Which finally brings us to that first "of course", the "of course, when we do so 'let Him do it'...then something changes in us". This is the second main point of our text: "you also were circumcised, in the putting off of (not a piece of skin, but) the (whole) sinful nature...When you were dead in your sins and in the uncircumcision of your sinful nature, God made you alive with Christ".

Before the trust came – either by the action of the Holy Spirit in Baptism or through the explained message ("faith comes from hearing the message" – Romans 10:17, if it comes later in life instead of as an infant) – before the trust came, we could do no spiritually good thing at all – we were "dead", unable to obey God. Sure, we could hear His commands and outwardly obey some of them (such as "do not murder" – although others, such as "always tell the truth", we could not obey). But our nature always said: My way! Not Your way, God! So, because of sinning we never could please God at all! We were dead – unable to do right and good, so we were doomed!

But by bringing us into the trust of letting Him do it His way, we now are released from the deadness of our sinful nature to be alive! To be able to obey Him!

Which is what we automatically begin to do as we trust His promise! "Automatically" we "begin", meaning: not fully, not completely – our sinful nature stubbornly keeps ruining our efforts – and sometimes gets the better of us so we give in to temptation even enthusiastically – for a while – until we come to our spiritual sense again. But the point of our text is: we no longer have to sin – we've been released from the iron grip of our sinful nature so we are now able – yes, *able* to obey Him as we never could while in unbelief, refusing to trust His promise.

This obeying, this living as the Lord commands, still needs the Holy Spirit's working in us – we need "food" for not only our faith (to remain in that trust) but also for our faithfulness (our obeying Him). This is why the Scriptures direct us to remember Baptism, to remember as we listen and read and think, to remember and receive in Holy Communion, to remember His promise in Jesus. This is how the Holy Spirit keeps working in us so that we not only trust, but also obey, that is: begin living daily not according to our sinful nature, but according to the godly nature He has given us.

And for specific directions in that godly living, please read the next paragraphs which the Holy Spirit inspired Paul to write: Colossians 2:16-3:17.

September 15, 2013

Theme: **Communion**

Related Reading: 1 Corinthians 11:23-32

Text: Matthew 26:17-30

THEIR PASSOVER – OUR COMMUNION

For the Old Testament people of God – including the time of Jesus, all the men, if possible, were to attend three great festivals at the temple in Jerusalem: the festival of Passover – which made them remember how God had delivered their nation physically from slavery in Egypt; the festival of Weeks – 50 days later, which was a thanksgiving day, both for the first harvest and for the giving of the Law to Moses on Mt. Sinai; and the festival of Booths – the fall thanksgiving day, when they especially thanked God for supplying them again with food for physical life, just as He had fed them for those forty years in the wilderness, when they lived in booths or tents. Of these three festivals Passover was the greatest – which is why so many pilgrims were in Jerusalem that last week of Jesus' earthly – in contrast to His resurrected – life. So the pilgrims came – with their families, if possible; yet not all could come – some had to stay home as guards for the villages, for example. But most came, bringing a special offering of thanksgiving.

The Passover observance, however, was not celebrated in the temple, because the Passover was a family – or a couple of families together, according to Exodus 12 – meal. It did have a very set ritual included to remember how the angel of death had in Egypt passed over every home of the

Israelites who in faith had smeared the blood of the sacrificed perfect lamb on the doorposts of their homes, a perfect lamb, which was the meat of that family meal. The sacrifice of a perfect lamb was also supposed to make them think of God passing over their sins in order to rescue them, though they didn't deserve it. It was for this festival family meal that Jesus and His disciples gathered.

To picture this, however, do not have in mind the familiar "Last Supper" painting by Leonardo da Vinci, because he got it wrong. They did not sit at a table, but, as our text says, they "reclined", stretched out on low couches, leaning on one elbow, as was the custom for festival meals. Leonardo painted the moment when Jesus announced that one of them would betray Him that night. Judas then immediately left, according to John 13, so he did not receive the first Holy Communion. Leonardo probably got the number of disciples wrong also, because, although our text does say Jesus was there "with the Twelve", Acts 1 implies that at least a few others were also there, because a successor to Judas had to be selected from "one of the men who have been with us the whole time the Lord Jesus went in and out among us, beginning from John's baptism to the time when Jesus was taken up from us" (Acts 1:21-22). Not that the total number is important, but it gives us a fuller picture of that last supper scene.

As a family meal, there would be plenty of talking – it was not a solemn quiet-as-a-church-mouse scene. And there was time, time for Jesus to wash their feet, to speak of His being betrayed, to teach them much about Himself as the only way to God – which involved His conversation with Thomas about His being "the way, the truth, and the life" so that "no one comes to the Father except through Me" (John 14: 6).

And there was time, not only for the Passover ritual words, but also for the institution of Holy Communion, which did not take place all at once, for at first, says our text, after having gotten their attention, "while they were eating, Jesus took bread, gave thanks and broke it, and gave it to His disciples, saying, 'Take and eat, this is My Body'". Then toward the end of the meal, as Luke writes: "In the same way, after the supper, He took the cup, saying: 'This cup is the new covenant in My blood'" (Luke 22:20).

Notice, Luke's words say: "This cup is the new covenant", while our text and also Mark's Gospel (14:24) say: "This is My blood of the covenant". Which is it exactly? Has to be that both are true, because these are direct quotes, somewhat different from each other, because wouldn't Jesus have to repeat Himself at least once or even more since His words were so shocking? Think of the look on the faces of the disciples – and probably their immediate whispers: What? His blood? How can that be? He's sitting there alive so how can this wine be His blood – for that matter, how could that bread which He broke be His body? Did we hear correctly? His Body – His Blood? So, knowing their questions, Jesus must have repeated Himself, in a sense saying: yes, this really is My Body, My Blood – and we are beginning the new covenant between God and sinners, the covenant sealed with the giving of My body and the shedding of My blood. The old covenant with Israel, although definitely pointing to the coming Sacrifice for sinners, still was worded primarily about this life, the "kingdom"; "My new covenant" is primarily about eternal life, "the kingdom of heaven".

Of course, they still didn't understand Jesus, in fact, couldn't understand, since they still didn't know how He was going to suffer and die – nor did they understand why, even after it happened. Which is why Jesus emphasized (according to Luke 22 and 1 Corinthians 11): "Do this in remembrance of Me" – remember, not only *what* happened in My whole life and especially in My suffering and death – remember *why* it happened: "the blood of the (new) covenant, poured out for many ("for you" according to Luke) for the forgiveness of sins". The new covenant is the declaration by God that He gives His forgiveness of sins, not on the basis of animal sacrifices or of physical descendancy, but strictly and only because of the sacrifice of His Son, the *truly* innocent Lamb of God.

Of course, it had always been this way – God forgave in the old Testament times because of the coming once-for-all Sacrifice, of which the repeated sacrificing of animals was to remind them. Now, however, it is so much clearer: forgiveness of sins is only because of Jesus' sacrifice of His Body, His Blood.

Which is the message of our Holy Communion, the successor to the Passover ceremony (as Baptism is the replacement for Old Testament circumcision, the declaration by God in a physical way: you belong to Me – I paid for you – don't ever leave). The message of Holy Communion clearly is: forgiveness has been earned and given by the sacrifice of the perfect Lamb of God, Jesus. Remember! Not by any works we have done! Only by the sacrifice of His Son! That's how our forgiveness has been won!

And it is a finished work! For Jesus said with His dying breath: "It is finished!" (John 19:30) – completed , paid, done! Forgiveness has been declared! There on that cross – on that day! Remember *this*! So that you trust only in what He did – there – for you – and for all sinners! Finished! Forgiven!

Which means that we do not get forgiveness when we receive His Body, His Blood. For forgiveness *is* ours, not because we do even such a little thing as eating a bit of bread and drinking a sip of wine. If that were the case, then we would have done something to get forgiveness, we would have earned it by our doing. No! Forgiveness has been proclaimed by Jesus there with His dying breath: Finished! The work is done! Forgiveness is declared for all sinners! And as you or I as individual sinners trust that what Jesus did was for you, for me, since we are helpless to get forgiven of our sins by ourselves – as we depend on what Jesus did, we benefit from what Jesus did, we receive the gift of God, forgiveness of our sins so we can have eternal life with Him!

Absolutely! Forgiveness is only because of Jesus, not because of communing! As Luther explained in the Small Catechism: "How can bodily eating and drinking do such great things? Certainly not just eating and drinking do these things, but the *words* written here: 'Given and shed for you for the forgiveness of sins.' These *words*, along with the bodily eating and drinking, are the main thing in the sacrament. Whoever *believes* these words *has* exactly what they say: 'forgiveness of sins'." Which means: if you do not have forgiveness through faith when you come up to communion, you will not have forgiveness, when you return to your pew, BECAUSE! Forgiveness is ours only through faith in Jesus, Who gave Himself as the true Passover Lamb of God so that God would pass over our sinning to keep us alive with Himself forever.

If so, then what's the point of receiving His Body, His Blood, in communion? For one thing, as Paul wrote to the Corinthians (11:26): "Whenever you eat this bread and drink this cup, you proclaim the Lord's death until He comes". That is, you confess your faith in Him for everyone to see: I am a sinner who *needs* forgiveness – I trust in Jesus Who *gives* me forgiveness by having given and shed this Body and this Blood for me.

But more than that confession is what He does for us in this sacrament. For here He literally touches us physically to assure us beyond doubt: no matter how guilty, I have taken away every single one of your sins, all the past and already even the sins to come. Peace, My child, peace!

And also, My child, I am with you – not only here in this touchable way, but also with you day by day to help you endure whatever attacks you, to help you remain in faith and faithful in living, for I am with you always as your Forgiver, as your Savior, as your Helper. So, have peace, My child; but also have courage, as you live for Me until I come for you.

Which is why we can depart from communion with joy to serve the Lord. We have His power to live faithfully *for* Him, because we do have peace *with* Him for Jesus' sake.

April 13, 2014

Theme: **Worship**

Related Reading: John 4:19-26

Text: Hebrews 12:28-29

WITH REVERENCE AND AWE

Which kind of worship service do you prefer: traditional liturgical, contemporary praise, or a combination? Many sincere Christians have quite strong opinions about which liturgy (for even the most contemporary praise service has a "liturgy", that is, a definite pattern in the service) *should* be used, which is the *right* one? Personally, I am convinced it doesn't matter – as long as the clear Christian message is proclaimed: the Law to make us admit again that we need a Savior, the Gospel which leads us to depend on Jesus as that Savior, and then the Law again to guide us in our thankful living. If that clear message is not preached, then that is not a **Christian** worship service at all! But if that message is being proclaimed, the "meat and potatoes" of the spiritual meal is clearly in the service, and "all the rest is just salad dressing" – which varies according to individual tastes.

Ah, ha, someone might say, however: but doesn't this very text which your message today is based on give us clear direction toward which type of service to have? For it says: "worship God acceptably with reverence and awe", and how can there be "reverence and awe" in a loud "praise service" with people clapping and swaying and almost shouting in keeping with the loud praise band music?

Well, it depends on your definitions! Not only the definition of "reverence" and "awe", but also of "worship God"! For if this verse is used to justify only the solemn liturgical type of service, how does that judge the types of worship services referred to in the Bible? The Old Testament service surely was not "solemn", not with its animal sacrifices and its "trumpet...harp and lyre...tambourine and dancing...strings and flute...clash of cymbals" according to Psalm 150 (which means, doesn't it, that a "praise band" is more Biblical than an organ for leading in worship). And the New Testament form of worship, as outlined according to 1 Corinthians 14, sure sounds more like a spirited Bible study group than a formal liturgy – it did have Scripture readings and preaching (according to 1 Timothy 4:13), which included reading the letters of Paul, but also included discussing what was preached and read. "Reverence and awe"? Not if those words mean "quiet and orderly"!

Actually, "reverence and awe" are inner attitudes more than they are outer actions – they refer primarily to why we are doing what we are doing more than how we are doing them.

Even more, what definition of "worship God" are we to use in this verse? A formal time of worship, instruction, and praise? But listen to St. Paul as he describes "worship", which according to the Greek word means what we do to serve God; in Romans 12 he was inspired to write: "Therefore, I urge you, brothers, in view of God's mercy, to offer your bodies as living sacrifices, holy and pleasing to God – which is your spiritual worship" (v.1). Which means that our "worship" of God takes place not primarily when we are gathered together with other Christians for a formal "service", but most of our worship of God, our service to Him, takes place when we are with non-Christians, when we are living our daily lives! Yes, the Greek word for "worship" does refer to "religious duties", but Paul expands that meaning to include all "service" to God, all week long, not just at a worship gathering. The fact is: if we do not "worship", serve, God in daily living, we can't actually "worship" Him when we gather for "worship"! "Faith without deeds is dead" (James 2:26 – but also vv.14-17) so that "Sunday worship" is merely hypocrisy if it is not "proven" (2 Corinthians 9:13) by how one serves God, lives for God, the rest of the week.

That being so, our text then is teaching about our inner attitude and motivation whenever or wherever we serve God, whether in daily living or in a formal religious gathering with fellow believers – we are to "worship (serve) God...with reverence and awe" – we are to do whatever we do, whether tell the truth or help someone or sing or listen to His message being proclaimed with the attitude of: how great God is – how much He has done and does for me – He is why I am doing now what I am doing.

Isn't this also what Jesus was meaning when He told the Samaritan woman at that well in John 4 that "the true worshipers will worship the Father in spirit and truth" (v.23)? True, a different Greek word is used here for whatever Aramaic word Jesus actually spoke, a Greek word which does refer more to religious formalities, but Jesus is primarily emphasizing the inner realities: "spirit and truth".

And that inner attitude of respect for and awe of God is to be caused, in the words of our text, by the fact that "we are receiving a kingdom that cannot be shaken". This is the "kingdom of heaven", as Jesus called it, or "life everlasting" or "eternal life" as He also called it (John 3:16). This "cannot be shaken" – it will last forever.

This is God's gift to us which we do not earn but only "receive", for it is what Jesus has paid for. Our sinning had shut us out as rebels against God. And even when we try to serve God instead of rebel against Him, we still have times of rebellion, when we insist on our way instead of His. Example: self-pity instead of trust! Which can be as innocent-sounding as "I'm getting sick of this recovery process – especially with ten more months until I've completely recovered" instead of patiently being thankful that God has made our bodies to be able to heal, even from the trauma of a broken hip as well as so much else. Or those so many times in daily living when, afterward, we have to pray: there I went again – forgive me – and help me, Lord! And to be in awe that He is so great that He does!

Sometimes, of course, life does not include a healing process: health is ending – a situation will not change. Then it is more difficult to have "reverence and awe" toward God.

Still, we can – and will have that, as we think again: this life is not the kingdom I'm meant for – the eternal, unshakable kingdom is coming – and it is mine, because Jesus earned it, even for me ("enough grace, even for you", remember?); so I am thankful for that gift to come in spite of the difficulties I now have to endure until that kingdom comes.

So, why do we serve God day by day and also in formal "praise-Him" times? Because of what He has done – for me – and for all sinners! Jesus has opened the way into His "kingdom of heaven", into "eternal life" – and the Holy Spirit has caused me to "receive" it by faith in Jesus, by trusting in His work only, not in any of my efforts to serve Him, to obey Him.

Our text adds a warning which we don't like to even hear – in fact, some theologians say: don't mention it, because we don't have to be afraid of God in the least, since we receive His love in Jesus. But God's Word says it so we have to realize its meaning for us: "our God is a consuming fire". God is serious about our serving Him instead of going our own way. We dare not think: this one little sin won't matter – partly because that thinking soon leads to: and this one is more serious, but it doesn't matter either and that soon leads to: doesn't matter what I do wrong, because God forgives all my sins. No! We dare not take God and His love for granted! That is not "reverence and awe" but rebellion – which our sinful nature keeps wanting to do! Which is why Luther's Catechism continually reminds us, our sinful nature: "We should fear and love God" (explanation to each Commandment) and "God threatens to punish all those who transgress these commandments; therefore we should fear His wrath" (Conclusion to the Commandments). Fear is not our motive; but our sinful nature will not lessen its efforts unless it hears these threats.

But Jesus in what He has done for us sinners is our true motive. That is why we are in "awe": that He would and could do that for me! That is why we are reverent, respectful, so we want to do what honors Him.

Which brings us back to public worship services! We all are different in what is meaningful for us. In my family two of the "kids" prefer praise worship liturgy, one prefers traditional. I myself could not survive spiritually, as I have told many, on only praise worship – even if the message was always clearly proclaimed ("praise music" too often has primarily repetition instead of instruction – but it is also personal preference). And it all is personal preference, as long as God's truth is proclaimed – also in the singing. If the motive is "reverence and awe", thanks for what Jesus has done for us, the form doesn't matter (although we have to recognize that formal liturgy can degenerate into mindless ritual, which is not worship at all, while some praise songs do not proclaim God's truth but merely glorify self).

So, which worship form should be used? Whichever form better communicates God's great message of forgiveness of sins through Jesus to the people who are attending. No point in arguing at all about the form – the content is all that really matters – for that Gospel content is what will help us truly worship/"serve" God day by day.

February 16, 2014

Theme: **Prayer**

Related Reading: Matthew 6:5-15

Text: Luke 18:1-8

PRAYER AS BATTERING RAM?

Bam! Bam! Bam! With practiced coordination the medieval soldiers rammed their battering ram against the castle gate – if they could just break through, they would conquer the nobleman and make him their slave! With enough men – and enough effort – it could be (and probably was) done back those centuries ago.

The way some people think about prayer sounds somewhat similar: if I pray enough and if enough other people are praying with me, then God will just have to do what we pray for! Isn't that what the parable in our text means? The widow kept at it until the judge gave in! And God's people are to "cry out to Him day and night" to get "justice", to get God to do the right thing for His people. Why Jesus even said that if only "two of you on earth agree about anything you ask for, it will be done for you by My Father in heaven" (Matthew 18:19). So, if you have a whole bunch of people praying with you for anything, God has got to give in and do it, doesn't He? Prayer as battering ram! Which would also apparently mean that through prayer you can force God to be your slave! To do whatever you want!

Huh? Can that be true? You can get the power through praying to force God to do your will no matter what He wants? That's what it sounds like the way many people think – and pray! Prayer as battering ram!

And so many people appear to believe this in our day that no wonder Jesus ends our text by saying: "However, when the Son of Man comes, will He find faith on earth?" For not only do so many people, church people, practice self-righteousness (which Jesus condemns in the parable right after our text); but also so many other church people practice the *I'm going to do what I want to do no matter what God's word says* attitude, such as: living in sexual immorality – which completely denies actual faith in Jesus: "those who live like this will not inherit the kingdom of God" (Galatians 5:21). With so many church people having sexual affairs while still claiming to be Christians and with so many other church people believing this battering ram idea of how to control God, how much faith is there any more in the organized church? And there is none outside the church (the church being, not organization, but the one family of all believers)! How much faith will He find when He returns?

For surely it is not "faith", as defined by Scripture, to think that prayer can make you more powerful than God! That is absolute rejection of God's teaching about prayer, about life, about Himself. Even Jesus, God on earth, prayed so fervently, as He faced the agony of suffering hell in our place: "Father, if You are willing, take this cup from Me; yet not My will, but Yours be done" (Luke 22:42). And as James wrote: "If it is the Lord's will, we will live and do this or that" (James 4:15). After all, regarding what plan should happen in our lives, which do you really prefer: the one we want or His? Who is wiser: the eternal, all-knowing God or small, limited sinful you or me? Obvious answer, isn't it?

So what is Jesus teaching here in our text and at other times, when He tells us to keep on praying? To understand this we need to understand clearly what prayer actually is. The essential definition of prayer is: talking with God – although it might be better understood as: talking things over with God. To talk things over with someone means that you have an idea and you want someone with more experience and wisdom to give you evaluation and guidance. If you don't want that help, then you just go to a "yes-man", who will agree to whatever you think! Then you are not "talking it over", but just telling someone, whom you consider inferior to yourself, what you are going to do.

But is God inferior and you superior? If that is your inner attitude or your prayer attitude, then you are not praying to God at all but are just "babbling...many (meaningless) words" (Matthew 6:7). Praying to God always is – has to be: I need Your help, Lord! I think this, I want that, but I don't really know what is truly good for me. So, please help me to understand and accept what You know and plan, Your will, Your plan for my present situation, for my life.

Which also applies when praying for others in their needs: yes, help them, Lord, but especially help them be accepting of how You are guiding – or allowing – in their life situation, whether illness, tragedy, or even happiness (help them remember to recognize their happiness is Your blessing, not their doing). The only exception to this request for help to see and accept His will, His plan, would be to thank Him for what He has done in my life, so that I humbly remember: His blessing, not my doing – although I have to use my time and abilities and effort to carry out His plan.

But it isn't easy, given our self-centered and proud natures, to accept or understand God's plan for us. That's why Jesus teaches: keep on praying, keep on until you get it! Get what? Your way? Did you listen carefully and notice what Jesus says is the promise in our text? "And will not God bring about justice for His chosen ones, who cry out to Him day and night?" "Justice" – as God determines it, of course! Which is another way of saying: "His will", isn't it? So actually Jesus could agree with the description of prayer as "battering ram" – not against God, but against our pride and selfishness and limited vision! Keep praying until you see God's plan working out – or until you truly want His plan, whatever that will be, in your life.

This attitude in prayer is based on one's humble trust that, a., God is greater and knows better than you do – as Jesus taught: "Your Father knows what you need before you ask Him" (Matthew 6:8), and, b., God always keeps His promises so that if He promises to work out what truly is good for you ("justice", our text says), He will do it.

And this humble trust is based on the first trust we have

in God: His love to forgive us all our sins because of Jesus and all He did as He was God on earth. That had been His promise ever since the first sin in that beautiful workplace, the Garden of Eden: the "offspring (or "Seed") of the woman (the man has to be included,too, of course) would "crush" the offspring of the one who first got those two humans to sin (Genesis 3:18). A rather vague promise, but it was given with increased clarity as the centuries and millenniums went by. His people looked for its fulfillment and wondered: how long? But finally God acted: "When the time had fully come, God sent His Son...to redeem those under the Law (condemned as sinners by God's Law) that we might receive the full rights of sons (Galatians 4:4-5). God kept His promise, this greatest one! We sinners could have no hope before His bar of justice! But by the actions of Jesus on earth, what He did and what He experienced, we receive God's justice, His forgiveness, His declaration: not guilty! We truly cannot understand how God can do that: "not guilty" when I am guilty? Yet He says: Because of Jesus! So, we trust that it is so! And it is!

And so, trusting that promise, we can trust His promise to work in us so we will see and accept and be a willing part of His will, His plan, in our lives. We realize that His will, His plan, might include pain and suffering on our part. But we can accept that, when it must be, as part of His plan which overall will be good for us, even in this life, but especially in eternal life, which is ours since we have been pronounced "not guilty" – "because of Jesus".

Which is why we don't have to feel guilty if we don't always pray with the correct attitude, such as only saying: I really need this, Lord (without any thought about "Thy will"); or if we don't pray every word with meaning. Those also are sins Jesus paid for and so He says to us: I took also that guilt to My cross for you, so just keep on praying – talk to Me about your concerns.

A final note: if God knows and has planned and we can't change Him but can only accept His plan, what's the point of talking over anything with God? He will do what He will do no matter what I think or say or do! But! He has commanded us to talk to Him, because in that talking, we will be remembering His promises and learning more to trust Him – which will help us more willingly participate in His plan.

To which we say: "Amen!" – which does not mean: "the end", but: "it will be, Lord, as You have promised!"

April 29, 2012

Theme: **Faith**

Related Reading: Hebrews 11:1-7

Text: Hebrews 11:8-10

FAITH: ABRAHAM'S AND OURS

If you meet someone new in the town where I live, Brookings, OR, a rather safe conversational question would be: "And where do you come from?" It seems as though most people here have come from somewhere else. They came for a variety of reasons: perhaps for a job, perhaps because relatives lived here, perhaps because of the ocean, perhaps because in vacationing they happened to come and just fell in love with the town and the ocean and the "banana belt" micro-climate which enables some flowers to blossom all year long. Plenty of reasons for coming.

Yet it's safe to assume that none of us had the reason for moving here that Abraham had for moving to his new place to live. For Abraham moved strictly because God told him to move to Canaan. That's what Genesis 12 (v.1) says: "The Lord had said to Abram, 'Leave your country, your people, and your father's household and go to the land I will show you'".

However, let's not overdo his moving "even though he did not know where he was going", as our text says. For he had almost moved there with his father some twenty or thirty years previously. As Genesis 11 says: "Terah took his son Abram...and they set out from Ur of the Chaldeans to go to Canaan. But when they came to Haran, they settled there" (11:31). Why had they wanted to move? Perhaps because they had heard that Canaan was a land "flowing with milk and honey", as the Israelites hundreds of years later were told by God (Exodus 3:8), kind of a "banana belt" reputation? However, after they had traveled about 600 miles, Terah stopped their move at Haran. Why? Maybe he got sick – or just sick of all the hassle in moving, for they didn't just pack up on a couple of camels, but had sheep and cattle and workers, quite a group – for when Abraham did finally move to Canaan, from what we learn of his wealth and male workers (318 were counted in his army a few years later to rescue Lot, his nephew, Genesis 14), perhaps a thousand people were involved. For whatever reason, Terah and his family, including Abraham, settled in Haran, where he eventually died about 100 years later.

But before Terah died, while Abraham (then called Abram, until renamed by God – Genesis 17) was prospering, God told him to move to Canaan, which was about 400 miles from Haran. In telling Abram to make this move, God also promised that his descendants would become "a great nation" and that "all peoples on earth will be blessed through you" (Genesis 12:2-3). So, Abram/Abraham did know something about Canaan, but he didn't know the details – he had never been there – so our text is correct in teaching that "by faith Abraham...went, even though he did not know where he was going": he knew the destination, but he didn't know the details. God said – he trusted – and he obeyed.

Our text adds a vital reason why he obeyed without knowing the details. Abraham knew that this life was not all there would be to his life. "For", as our text says, "he was looking forward to the city with foundations, Whose architect and builder is God", which "city" was, as further explained in some verses after our text, "a better country – a heavenly one" (v.16). Some teachers in our day say that people in the Old Testament times had no concept of a personal eternal life. This chapter in Hebrews teaches that they did! They looked forward to eternal life , as we do.

Of course, it was not as clear to Abraham and the other Old Testament believers about exactly how they would receive that promised "city" or "country". They didn't ever hear the name "Jesus" (although the name "Joshua" in Hebrews means "God saves" which is also what "Jesus" in Greek essentially means), and they didn't – couldn't – have a clear understanding of that death on that specific cross with that Jesus being the way to eternal life. But they had promises which made them realize: somehow – some day – God would send Some One – so all people could be blessed. The specific promise about this which Abraham had was not only the one in Genesis 12 that "all peoples on earth will be blessed through you", but what God later promised him: "Through your offspring (or "seed") all nations on earth will be blessed" (Genesis 22:18), which meant that through one particular Descendant this blessing for all would come – Some One would come and be God's way to bring blessing.

So, the faith of Abraham, which St. Paul especially in the book of Romans praised as the best example of what faith continues to be even for us in the New Testament, since Jesus, that Some One, has come and completed His work of opening the way to the "city with foundations", the "better country", which we usually refer to as eternal life, the faith of Abraham is also to be our faith, faith which is not merely words of believing, but faith which is trusting what God says so that we obey what He says, even if we don't know exactly where that obedience will lead us.

That faith really has two parts to it. The first part is about the final destination and how we get there – the second part is about the journey we will have in getting there. As Abraham trusted for that ultimate destination, so do we. Abraham realized that he couldn't get there on his own – he didn't deserve it – that's why he made sacrifices: I've sinned – You, Lord, have to forgive. And he believed, he trusted, that God did forgive, did give this blessing, which would finally be based on that coming Some One. So we also trust – in Jesus – for forgiveness – which gives us that eternal life. There is a command in this which is to be obeyed: the *only* way is through Jesus – never let your pride distract you – trust only in Jesus, nothing of yourself. That is your faith – and mine – right? Jesus paid my way – by His perfect living and by His total suffering. This part of faith's obedience has no unknown quantity to it. Trusting in Jesus **is** the way to eternal life.

But faith is not a paid-for ticket which one hides away in

the wallet of one's mind until the entrance gate is reached; faith is on daily display all along the way to that final destination. Which means that, like Abraham, the second part of our faith is that we are to trust and obey whatever the Lord might say even though we can't know the details of what will happen along the way.

Abraham, of course, had direct verbal, back and forth conversation with God. We have His written Word instead, which does not give us detailed instructions as Abraham received, but gives us the guideline principles for living in summary commands, such as, be honest, be kind, forgive, be faithful, be thankful, pray, do what is right no matter the consequences from those who want to do wrong, take time every day privately and especially every week publicly to receive the assurance of His forgiveness and the directions of His guidance from His Word.

These are not always easy to obey, since our lives in this sinful world experience so many pressures and temptations – and our sinful natures don't want to obey, especially since we easily are afraid of how life will turn out if we do what God says instead of what we want.

That's why we always need to keep in mind what faith really is: faith is trust in God's love for us, His love proven by the work of His Son Jesus for us, His love which promises: do as I say, and your life will be better for you according to My standards, since I truly know what is better for you.

Which leads us to confess to Him as we remind ourselves: I trust You, Lord, for my eternal destination:; therefore, help me daily trust Your commands for my life and follow them as best I can, until I get there.

June 15, 2014

Theme: **Hope**

Related Reading: Romans 8:18-25

Text: **1 Peter 1:17-21**

HOPE! INSTEAD OF EMPTY!

Not long ago Marian and I watched a Netflix movie about a woman whose life was empty. She had just been released from prison after serving 15 years for having murdered her six-year-old son. Although she had "paid her debt to society", she could not escape what she had done. As the movie unfolded, I expected it would end in her suicide, because her life was so empty; and, since it was a French film, there was not even a hint of any message about forgiveness being available to give her even a ray of hope. But it ended with her just accepting what she did and the burden she had to remember. Still an empty life, but at least a life.

It doesn't take such a horrific deed to give a person an empty life with no hope. An abortion, which in fact is almost as horrific, does that to some women, no matter what the perverted teachings of pro-abortionists say. A significant number of women bear that endless guilt which makes living feel empty, because: "I killed my baby!" Which guilt can be lifted through the clear message of forgiveness for all our sins, no matter how horrific – but it usually takes a life-wrenching journey until the woman actually believes: "Yes, He gave His life because I took my baby's life – so He does forgive me."

But an empty life can be felt also because of far less serious reasons. Even the natural death of a loved one, let alone a tragic, unexpected death, can take away one's hope in living – life can seem so empty without that loved spouse – or child. Or when facing one's own death, inevitable as death is, but coming so definitely – emptiness – what's the point of still living at all? That empty feeling can come regarding dying, not only because of illness but just because of age. Life can seem empty-- if there is no hope.

And still lesser reasons can cause that empty feeling in people: life just isn't going well, perhaps, or, stuck in a rut with no end in sight, or, so lonely, nobody cares, and more reasons. So many millions of Americans have that empty life condition. Why else do they flee into alcohol or drugs or continual excitement or unthinking entertainment or riotous fanatical mobs or sex except to escape the dreariness, the emptiness of their lives? And now with the legalization of marijuana in so many states how much more escapism will take place? There apparently are some legitimate medical marijuana usages, but mostly it's just to get high enough to not have to think about the emptiness of the reality of life, when there is no real hope.

Our text teaches us instead about hope, the hope we can have, no, the hope we DO have because of Jesus. Peter wrote – by inspiration, of course: "You know that it was not with perishable things such as silver or gold that you were redeemed (that is, set free) from the empty way of life handed down to you from your forefathers." The Greek word, translated here as "empty", has the idea of "pointless, all in vain" (like Solomon wrote in Ecclesiastes). Which is the "way of life" handed down from generation to generation. An alcoholic parent so often raises alcoholic children – not always, but often. A family which feeds on hatred of another family or another nationality will have grandchildren with that same hatred – the feuding of the Hatfields and McCoys is not totally fictional – and feuding continues no matter how much heartache it produces, let alone broken bones and deaths. "The empty way of life" feeds on itself, whether in families or just in one's own mind!

But it doesn't have to! That's Peter's assurance, his "good news"! We have been "redeemed" from that emptiness, that hopelessness, so we don't have to experience it at all or continue in it, if we have fallen into it. We can't end it by ourselves – can't just tell ourselves: don't feel that way – find something useful to do! That's what Solomon tried – but he wrote that it didn't work – and Scripture indicates that he never escaped it, even though he taught that God, the true God, was the only way for hope and meaning. He tried to do it himself – but he failed. "As Solomon grew old, his wives turned his heart after other gods...so Solomon did evil in the eyes of the Lord...the Lord became angry with Solomon because his heart had turned away from the Lord" (1 Kings 11:4-9). Nor can any of us "buck up" by ourselves to have hope instead of emptiness.

BUT! "You were redeemed...with the precious blood of Christ, a lamb without blemish or defect" – He lived a perfect life! "He was chosen before the creation of the world, but was revealed in these last times for your sake" – Jesus was God's eternal plan so we sinners could have hope in spite of our rebellions against God, which in themselves would destroy all hope and put us into the emptiness of eternal damnation.

So Jesus came – and lived perfectly – and shed His innocent blood (another way of saying: "His innocent life") so that we could have hope – and: life with meaning and purpose. As we have heard this explanation of the meaning of Jesus' life and work, we have come to faith in Him as our Savior, as Peter explains: "Through Him (Jesus) you believe in God Who raised Him from the dead and glorified Him so that your faith and hope are in God" – which means: there are so many "gods", false gods – everyone believes in a "god" of some sort – even atheists betray their belief when they say: "God damn it" or "by God" – even evolutionists, who actually are atheists, believe in a "god": the god of matter, which has always existed – and naturalists worship Gaea, Mother Earth – everyone believes in some kind of "god".

But none of these "gods" are real! And so they do not give any "hope", any confidence about one's personal future. The true God, the only actual God, is the One Jesus revealed, the God of grace, that is, of undeserved love Who forgives, the God of mercy, the God Who does not revel in killing as the Islamic Allah does, but the God Who wants to save and to bless – forever! This is the God Jesus revealed by His life and work! Actually, this is how Jesus revealed Himself, since He is truly "Immanuel", "God with us", God come to earth. So Peter explains: as you have believed in Jesus "your faith and hope are in God", not in false gods, but in the one true God, the one and only God.

So, our "faith" is that we trust in what God has done for us – our "hope" is that we trust in what He will do with us. He has forgiven us – He has set us free (redeemed us) to be able to "live (our) lives as strangers here in reverent fear" – and He promises that we shall live with Him eternally, not as "strangers" but as His dear people.

Two things at this point: we know and trust what He has done – that is faith; "hope" is that we believe and trust what He will do; but since that is in our future, not our present reality, it is called our "hope", our trust in His promises for the future.

Which means, second of all (have to explain this first so that we have courage and commitment to do the "first of all"), there is a future planned for us by our God, a home that will be with Him at first temporarily (don't be shocked – we confess this every week in the Creeds) in a spiritual existence in His Presence (we call this "heaven"); then will come the Last Day for this universe, to be replaced with the perfect, never-to-be-marred-by-sin new creation which we will enjoy in our resurrected, our re-created bodies (the Creed says: "resurrection of the body", doesn't it?). That's God's promise for our future – assured to us by what Jesus did, as He lived on earth, as He suffered and died on the cross.

Which brings us to the "first of all": our future is not just after we die. Our future is our living this life until we die. That's why Peter writes: "Live your lives as strangers here with reverent fear". This does not mean we try to escape life in this sinful world – can't! But because we keep our true God in mind, because we keep Jesus in mind – that's "reverent fear" – we live as His people, who are different from those who are hopeless. Because of our "hope", our trust in His eternal promises, as well as our trust that He is with us to help us and guide us and protect us (for these are His promises also for our future living, our living day by day), we will live His way, as best we can – we are "in but not of this world", for we are His. And our purpose, which gives meaning to living – is to do what pleases Him instead of what gratifies our sinful natures. So can we live lives which are kind and helpful to others. And in that way of living we find that life never is empty, but has meaning and satisfaction, for that, too, is part of His promise as we live out our future.

Our future in this life may not be long – none of us knows how long. But we will find satisfaction in living it, because we will be doing what we can to obey and serve the only true and living God.

June 22, 2014

Theme: **Love**

Related Reading: John 13:31-35

Text: 2 John 1-6

LOVE: NOT FEELING BUT HELPING

Most of us, I'm pretty sure, when we hear the word "love", almost automatically think "feeling". Which makes the request in our text ("I ask") quite uncomfortable for us, even though it is based on Jesus' command: "love one another" (John 13:34). Not only too many people to "love", but some of even our fellow believers are just not very appealing people – not only because of some sinning they have been guilty of, but also because of their personalities or appearances or even how they smell. After all, since we still have our sinful nature, those factors do influence us so that I don't like every other Christian and not all of them like me! No, John! No, Jesus! You can't expect me to feel positively about all of them! No way!

Well, there is an easy way out of this reluctance on our part – and this is the actual point of our text. The "love" Jesus commands is not feeling, but obeying – obeying His commands to be kind and helpful to others in their needs no matter how we feel about them. As our text says plainly: "This is love: that we walk in obedience to His commands". Love is not feeling but doing – obeying God in how we treat one another.

Since that's the essential truth of this text and of this

specific "Message from the Coast", I suppose that, if you are really busy this week, you could quit reading right now and get to your other activities.

If so, however, you would never truly be "walk(ing) in love" as our text says. For just as no one can command you to have feeling love for another person, no one, not even Jesus, can just command us to do what we are supposed to do and expect us to do it. That's why Jesus always teaches about what He is doing for us so that faith is worked more fully in us – then faith will show our thanks, which will be guided by His commands. That's why Jesus phrased His command, as He did, on that Maundy Thursday when He said: "As I have loved you, so you must love one another." He's not saying: "I'm setting you an example", but: I'm giving Myself as Sacrifice for your sins so that not only are you forgiven, but also you are set free from the necessity of sinning. This is also why our text repeatedly emphasizes "the truth", as John addresses this house congregation directly and us by application: "I love in the truth...all who know the truth...because of the truth, which lives in us and will be with us forever...walking in the truth". "The truth" is the message of Jesus being the only Savior. To read this text is to be reminded of Jesus, Who is "the way, the truth, and the life" as He Himself taught (John 14:6).

Actually, all the New Testament books are written according to this principle: instruction about the life and work of Jesus to "redeem" us sinners, that is, to rescue us from the deserved consequences of our sinning and to set us free from sin's hold on us so that we are better able to obey the instructions for living that are then given. This is why, especially when we read the letters of Paul, we see how he always teaches about Jesus and His work. Was this all brand-new informational instruction which the original readers had never heard before? Hardly! For Paul is repeating the essentials of the gospel message, which he had first preached to them, in order to bring them to faith in Jesus. He repeats it in order to not only remind them of it, but to keep them in that faith, because they – we, also – have such sinful nature reluctance to keep believing it. Mostly it's our pride that doesn't want it, although at times our guilt makes us hesitant to believe it. However, did you ever notice that pride and guilt are two sides of the same coin of rejection? Pride says: I'm too good to need Jesus – guilt says: I'm too bad for Him to help me – I, I, I!

So, the Holy Spirit's method to work in us to better obey God's commands is to work in our "heart" (actually, of course, in our brains, but deeper than mere superficial thinking) to smash our pride in what we think we've done good and our pride in what we know we've done wrong (because actually, to claim our guilt is too much to be forgiven is to be proud – in a way – of what we've done: I'm worse than anyone else – and so, since I'm so bad that I can't be forgiven, I can't be helped to change – so I'll just have to keep on doing that particular sin or keep on berating myself for some past evil). Which is why the Holy Spirit works through this message about what Jesus did (the "gospel") and why He did it (the "law" – which points out our need for Him to so work) to keep us admitting: I can't – You did – I'll let You (as a shut-in friend of mine put it recently)! The "I'll let you" part of that phrase isn't precisely accurate, but it is how it feels to us when the Holy Spirit convinces us.

And He has to keep convincing us day by day, week by week, because we can so easily lose our trust in Jesus by falling into the ditch of self-righteousness or into the ditch of despair leading to evil living. That's why He always inspired the Scripture writers to review, to repeat, to teach again the message of Who Jesus is, what He did, and why He did it. As we think about it – as we go through the process of re-hearing it, our faith is refreshed, re-affirmed, so that we both want to and are more able to thank God for the "grace, mercy and peace" He gives us in Jesus, thank Him by trying to obey Him better.

And so, by repeatedly reminding his readers – including us – of "the truth" of Jesus, John helps us become more able to "walk in love", that is, "walk in obedience to His commands".

Which commands are the positive ones of what we are to do – which will keep us away from disobeying the "don't do" commands also. Actually, can't every command of God be understood in a positive "do this" way? "Don't commit adultery" means: keep sex holy, especially by being faithful in marriage – "don't murder" means: help others instead of hurting them – "don't steal" means: work for what you need and share, because the Lord will provide enough. Jesus summarizes all of the God's commands into the single word: "love" – using the Greek word (which translates whichever Aramaic or Hebrew word He actually used) which means: divine love – helping, kindness.

So, if you've read this far in this "Message", do you see why the Holy Spirit wants us to think through whatever Scripture He presents to us? This is why He set up the church to be primarily about preaching: so that the words of Scripture could be explained and applied so that the individual sinners would think about Jesus and His work again so that their trust in Him would continue and grow.

Which is why also the Holy Spirit's process includes specific repeating of the commands of God: faith never is all alone – receiving assurance of forgiveness always makes us give thanks – by deeds as well as in words – but we need to be guided specifically because our sinful nature really wants to only take, while still doing what it wants. Same way with our Christian hope, our trust in God's promises about our future still on earth and our eternal future: our sinful nature wants to say only: goody, goody, look what I'm going to get – instead of responding: because I know what He promises, I'll follow the guidance of His commands, even if I don't know what that might get me into. We need to be reminded of how we will show our thanks, as we live.

And in this text, the Holy Spirit is teaching and reminding and enabling us to "walk in love" – to live with kindness and helpfulness to all others as much as possible, but, as the Holy Spirit also teaches (Galatians 6:10), "especially to those who belong to the family of believers". We can, because He has worked in us, as we thought about His message also in this "Message".

June 29, 2014

Theme: **Trust**

Related Reading: Matthew 6:25-34

Text: Isaiah 30:15-18

RESTFUL TRUST OR RESTLESS WORRY

700 years before the birth of Jesus the Israelites faced a terrible threat: the Babylonians were set to completely conquer them! The Lord promised them: Trust Me – and I'll take care of you! But the Israelites said: No! We have to find a practical means of defense, even if it means to flee, "flee on swift horses", says our text. They should have trusted the Lord's promise, for not too long before He had protected them in King Sennacherib's war, killing 185,000 besieging soldiers overnight by "the angel of death" so that he retreated and left them alone. But, no! That they forgot (or thought: couldn't happen miraculously again) so they relied on an alliance with Egypt instead of relying on the Lord's promise. Result? Disaster! And the 70-year Babylonian Captivity for all the Israelite leaders and most of the population so that the land of Palestine was left almost deserted.

What can we learn for our lives right now from this little history lesson? God has promised to care for us, to provide for us, day by day, so He says: Don't worry – trust Me to provide for you, take care of you – no matter what seems to be threatening – trust Me and rest easy.

But we don't, do we! We take the short-term promise of

the Lord about providing food and drink and clothing (as Jesus teaches in the Sermon on the Mount, Matthew 6:25-34) for granted – for do any of us truly wonder what we will have to eat today or are any of us dressed in rags – but it's the long-term things that we worry about. And there is plenty of that long-term stuff threatening! As homosexuals continue their push to dominate public life, for that's what it is, not merely civil equality but dominance – have you heard there is now an effort to move or boycott the next Winter Olympics because Russia has banned "homosexual propaganda"? Evil will never be satisfied! And so there will be a push to ban even Bible verses by churches against homosexuality as "hate speech" in spite of constitutional protections for freedom of worship and of speech. Don't believe me? It is happening already in Canada and Sweden! "What kind of a country will we become?" can be our worry – and how will it affect especially our grandchildren?

And "Obamacare" with its effects! How much more will it cost us individually? Some states predict health insurance increases of 50 to 70% And federal employees in D.C. are reported as having complained they can't afford it! If they can't with their $70,000 and more incomes, what about us, especially us on Medicare? And how will health rationing, fueled by the lack of money and of doctors, affect us?

Or more personal for us who are aging: will I end up with Alzheimer's and a meaningless life? Or die very painfully? What is going to happen to me? Sure, Lord, short-term is easy, but what about long-term? And we worry – and lose sleep over our worries, not only these larger things, but about many lesser things: will I lose my job? will I have enough money to keep my home? will I be safe from criminals and con artists? how will my kids or grandkids turn out? So much to worry about!

So pointless! And so unnecessary! "Pointless", because what can you and I do to prevent any of these disasters? Yes, we can economize financially regarding some things, and we can try to eat more healthfully, but if Alzheimer's or other dementia is in your future or mine, there is nothing at all we can do to prevent it. In fact, the more we worry about something, the more likely it will happen, because we will use up restless energy and get less sleep and, therefore, will be less able to deal with whatever dreadful thing might happen. Worrying is "pointless"! It doesn't help at all!

And worrying is "unnecessary"! Because we have the Lord's promise to provide, to provide for us each day that comes, so He directs us to be concerned primarily about today, to live as faithfully as we can for Him according to His way today – and then tomorrow when that day comes – but today is to be our primary concern and effort – with the trust that, as He is providing sufficiently for us today, so He will day by day.

Which, of course, does not mean that we use no common sense and make no plans about tomorrow – and longer. We cannot be reckless today to spend all our resources and energy today so that we have nothing at all tomorrow. Our

Creator Lord, for example, provides bountiful gardens usually so that produce can be preserved in the fall for eating during the winter – which has to be translated for those of us, who have no garden or not enough garden to provide for all winter, into the principle that we do have to save some now to live on later – and to spend wisely what we do have. Still, not to make an idol out of food or money but to plan reasonably and wisely, trusting that He will provide as He has promised. But the main point is: do as wisely as we can, also in planning; but primarily live today in thankfulness with trust for the coming tomorrow. For is not this what Jesus is teaching in the prayer He taught? "Give us this day our daily bread": thanks for providing for us today and trust He will do so "daily".

But, still, things can be so worrisome! Dangers threaten – life is precarious – and we may not live to see tomorrow (or the next day or the next year), for death can come so quickly, even to God's children, to us! Which is why God through Isaiah in our text included His other promise, His greater promise, His eternal promise: "Yet the Lord longs to be gracious to you, He rises to show you compassion. For the Lord is a God of justice. Blessed are all who wait for Him!" "Gracious...compassion...justice", words about forgiveness actually – yes, even "justice" is about forgiveness. For how can there be forgiveness from God if there is no justice by God? Which is the promise of God to work out justice for us sinners, not by thundering His justice upon us – for then we would not survive to receive forgiveness; but by striking His Son on the cross with the lighting bolt of His justice, making Him endure all the punishment His justice requires for our sinning. Jesus' cross, that lonely "flagstaff on a mountaintop", that isolated "banner on a hill", was like a lightning rod to protect us sinners. It all hit Him! So that! As we hide in the narrow shelter of His cross, not letting any of our supposed goodness be exposed, for it is only "supposed" by us but would be condemned by God, so, as we hide in the narrow shelter of His lightning rod cross, trusting only in His enduring it all for us, not trusting in self or anything else, we are safe. That is the "gracious" attitude of God to us – that is His "compassion" for us, His "justice" for us: we deserve His punishment – we get instead His blessing.

And it is in that trust, that trust in His truly long-term promise, His promise of eternal life for all who hide in the shelter of Jesus, that we can be confident of His short-term promise of providing for us today, which then turns into His next-term promise of "daily" providing throughout life. True, He does not prevent all suffering from coming into our lives – some of His children even starve to death – and more of His children suffer oppression, even violence, when they live faithfully according to His Word. And also true: He does not prevent dementia or cancer or other dreadful health conditions from affecting some of His faithful children. But if any of these tragic things do finally happen to any of us, we can still be thankful for how He provided until then – and still is providing enough strength and endurance until

He finally calls us to Himself.

For that is the ultimate blessing and promise, isn't it? We want the best life we can have in this time of living. But eternal life with all its blessings is much more our "want", isn't it? And that is something we don't have to worry about. For that is His absolute promise in Jesus. Sure, we have to keep trusting in Him – day by day – so we don't fall away from faith by anti-Scriptural believing (including self-righteousness, trusting self instead of Jesus) or evil living. But as we keep hearing His promise in Jesus as well as His promise to provide for us daily, we can rest at peace: He will provide for us now – He will take us into eternal life – because of Jesus!

Thank You, Lord – and help me turn from the worry I so easily give in to so that I will have more restful trust – whatever I think might be coming into my life or the lives of those I love. Amen.

August 11, 2013

Theme: **Live in Peace**

Related Reading: Matthew 5:21-26

Text: Proverbs 3:27-32

TIPS FOR LIVING IN PEACE

"To live in peace" – isn't that what we all want, peace in our family, in our neighborhood, in our church, in our country? Then why don't we have that peace? Why is there so much conflict and unrest? Because we also have other "wants", things we want to have, things we want to do; and although sometimes we can find ways to peaceably get what we want and do what we want, all too often my want conflicts with your want so we have hurt feelings and hurtful deeds instead of peace. James wrote by inspiration: "What causes fights and quarrels among you? Don't they come from your desires that battle within you? You kill and covet, but you cannot have what you want. You quarrel and fight" (4:1-2). And that truth underlies the lack of peace on all levels, whether family, church, community, nations: I want – and insist on trying to get what I want! That's our sinful human nature!

But we do want peace – so, what can we do to have and enjoy peace? Are there any tips so we can achieve more peace in our lives? Our text from Proverbs gives some tips, but not the most important one – the one which deals with our wants!

It is not wrong to want a thing or an activity. That's just

part of life. If we didn't want, we wouldn't do. But the problem comes when we want it too much, when we think: I have to have or have to do this – no matter what! Which betrays a lack of trust in our God and Savior. For when we want something too much, we are saying: My will – no matter what You say, Lord, no matter what Your plan is for me. Instead of trusting that the Lord will provide enough for us, especially what is good for us, we insist like a spoiled little kid: my way!!!

That attitude is also behind every sin that we commit. God commands: Do this – but we say: No! My way! So we are in conflict with God every time we sin. And we would have no peace with God, if He had not acted to make peace by the sacrifice of His Son for us. For we are encircled by, trapped in, our sinning – no way we can break free from sinning and its consequences in this life – and even if we could miraculously stop sinning from this moment on, what about all that past sinning? We can't just say: Oh, forget those things, Lord, because, see how good I am now? Anyway, the facts are: can't totally stop present sinning and can't erase past history.

We can't – but He did! In Jesus God ended our war against Him, well, we should say: ended our state of war against Him. He never has been at war with us sinners – He always has loved all of us sinners, the whole world and history of sinners, so that finally He sent His Son to make it possible for us to be at peace with Him – in total fact although not in every detail – meaning: we can be at peace with Him, because Jesus has purchased us free from our sins, even though we do keep sinning daily – yet not with the wilfulness that we had before coming to faith (or returning to faith, as some of us have experienced). Those who do not trust in Jesus as their only way into peace with God are still captured by their sins with eternal consequences. But when we trust in Jesus as our Peace-Maker, then we have the Holy Spirit working in us to struggle against sinning.

And it is an on-going struggle – as our "wanting too much" proves! Which disturbs our peace with others who want too much also.

So, how to lessen the conflict in order to have more peace with others? The main "tip" God's Word gives is: trust Him to provide enough for you – trust Him to provide good for you – trust Him to provide what is good for you – even if it isn't what you think you want. Perhaps His clearest promise for this is as Paul wrote in Romans: "He Who did not spare His own Son, but gave Him up for us all – how will He not also, along with Him, graciously give us all things?" (8:32), which assurance followed the assurance: "We know that in all things God works for the good of those who love Him" (8:28). So, if we trust Him in Jesus for our eternal good, we can also trust Him for our good in living now.

Which is how we are to evaluate our "wants" when they come into conflict with the "wants" of others: I don't have to insist on my way, my plan, my desire – the Lord will provide fine for me, even if I give up my present "want" so the other person can have his/her "want". As God says in His Word: "Do nothing out of selfish ambition or vain conceit, but in humility consider others better than yourselves. Each of you should look not only to your own interests, but also to the interests of others" (Philippians 2:3-4).

Of course, we also have to evaluate what the other person wants, whether it is legitimate or strictly selfishness or otherwise sinful. We are not looking to their true "interest", if we are enabling them to sin. Say you have a $20 bill and want to go out for pizza – an alcoholic friend wants $20 to buy liquor – you dare not give him/her that $20 bill to aid him/her in sinning (instead, how about taking him/her along for pizza?). Again, it is not helping children or grandchildren to give them everything they want or allow them to do only what pleases them even though saying "No" most likely will produce conflict. But conflict can't always be avoided no matter how much we prefer peace; we have to do right and good even if conflict results.

Still, we need to try to live in peace, as Paul also wrote in Romans: "If it is possible, as far as it depends on you, live at peace with everyone" (12:18). And our verses from Proverbs give us some practical tips about how to do so.

Proverbs tip #1: "Do not withhold good from those who deserve it when it is in your power to act. Do not say to your neighbor: 'Come back later; I'll give it tomorrow' – when you now have it with you" – which means: do good to others whenever they need it and we are able to help. Which may mean that we may have to change what we are now doing, because help is needed now! To delay is to show: you are not very important to me – to delay, when we could take the time to help now, is also to imply: go ask someone else, don't bother me. Which does not make that person feel very good about us nor willing to help us if we have a need or a want. But truly helping will usually improve that person's attitude toward us so they will be more likely to try to get along with us in peace.

Of course, if that person is just selfishly trying to take advantage of us, the relationship will deteriorate rather than improve. Which is why the verse refers to "those who deserve (the good you can give)" – do they have a real need or are they just looking for an easy way to get what they want? Our responsibility is to truly "help" – that is what promotes a peaceful relationship.

Tip #2: "Do not plot against your neighbor, who lives trustfully near you. Do not accuse a man for no reason – when he has done you no harm." This is the flip side to tip #1: we are not to try to take advantage of those we live with, whether by trying to cheat them or by trying to harm them so we can gain advantage over them. It's not wrong to ask for help in our needs or even in our wants. In fact, if they do truly help us by working with us, they will feel better about knowing us. As helper and helpee share in working out a solution, they both are more likely to become more friendly and wanting to live in peace.

Tip #3: "Do not envy a violent man or choose any of his ways, for the Lord detests a perverse man, but takes the upright into His confidence." Let no one pretend that watching violent movies or playing violent computer games will not have a negative effect on the watcher or gamer. If violence thrills our vision and fills our mind, it will show itself in our daily living so that we will be more likely to try to force our way on others rather than be willing to help. There used to be a computer shorthand maxim: GIGO, meaning: garbage in, garbage out. If our minds feed on violence and force, our lives will eventually show it, for our attitudes will become hardened against others to just get for self, even if force or violence is needed. No peace in life that way!

We will never have a completely peaceful life here on earth. No matter how hard we try to live in peace by acting with kindness to help others and not trying to selfishly take advantage of others and not trying to get our way by force, sin always seeps into the situation, our sin ("me first!") and the sin of others ("no, me first!"). Which is why we need to keep coming back to the peace we have with God in spite of our sinning. For in His peace we also have power to try to avoid our own selfishness in order to help others so that we can have more peaceful relationships with the people we live with and among.

July 28, 2013

Theme: **Forgiving**

Related Reading: Matthew 18:21-35

Text: Luke 17:3-5

FORGIVE AGAIN? AND AGAIN?

Realistically, can you even imagine happening what Jesus said in our text? To have your brother – or your sister – hurt you somehow seven times in one day, each time apologizing and asking forgiveness, but then within an hour or so hurting you again? Couldn't do it – not in real life – not what Jesus said: "If he sins against you seven times in a day, and seven times comes back to you and says, 'I repent', forgive him." No, it could never happen; first, because if a brother – or sister – was so insensitive and so uncaring as to repeatedly sin against you, why would they even care whether you forgave them or not? And second, no ordinary person, even a person of faith in Jesus to be forgiven, could possibly do it! Once or twice, but seven times in one day? Forgive again – and again? Seven times? Impossible!

And yet, the disciples knew that Jesus never said anything He didn't mean – and the disciples knew that Jesus was especially emphatic about forgiving people. They probably remembered from His "Sermon on the Mount" when Jesus had taught that God could not forgive their sins against Him, if they would not forgive others who sinned against them. And it had been probably only a few weeks previously that Jesus had said they were to forgive others not just seven times but seventy times seven times, in other words: don't keep count! Just as God doesn't keep count against you (Matthew 18:21-35)! So, realizing how impossible it seemed to them to be able to forgive the same person on the same day seven times, their response was: "Increase our faith!" We could never do this without Your extra help through a deeper faith than we now have!

Which we today have to echo! We know how hard it is to forgive someone even once if he or she has deeply hurt us, whether emotionally, physically, or financially – but more than once? Even seven times in one day? The only way we are able to truly forgive someone at all is by remembering how much God has forgiven us! He has forgiven all our sins, our thousands and thousands of sins, so that, humbled by that fact accomplished through Jesus' sacrifice for us, we are able to forgive the relatively few, though painful, sins someone has hurt us with. And for repeated forgiving of others, we will have to be even more aware of and thankful for God forgiving us. Still will be a terrible emotional struggle, but we can forgive again – and again, because God forgives us again and again, every sin of every day.

And how is it that God can forgive us so completely? Because of Jesus – and what Jesus did! In one place – it's in 2 Corinthians 5 – God tells us through St. Paul: "God was reconciling the world to Himself in Christ, not counting men's sins (women's also, children's also) against them ... God made Him (Jesus) Who had no sin to be sin for us so that in Him we might become the righteousness of God" (vv.19,21). God has counted all our sins, every single one, also every evil done by all people, counted them up, even in advance, as though we humans were by sinning piling up a bankrupting spiritual debt – no way out – eternally bankrupt! But God charged all that debt to Jesus – and made Him pay! The payment being: perfect life and total punishment! Now, as we by faith are "in Him", it is almost kind of a spiritual identity theft! By faith we are saying: look at Jesus as though He was doing our sinning – and look at me as though I was as innocent as Jesus truly is! And God says: Right! You are righteous – in My sight! Forgiven! Without debt to Me! Because of Jesus!

Which forgiveness changes us! Now, instead of angrily trying to make that person pay or trying to get even with him or her, we also can say: I forgive you! I will not hold this against you! We can do that! Awfully difficult at times, but we can, as we remember how God forgives us, because He keeps working in us to please Him by doing what is right and good – which in this situation is: forgiving!

Hmm, but what is forgiving? Does that action include not only a handshake but a hug? Not only canceling a loan but immediately giving another one? Not necessarily! The hug might be needed, but another loan, more good money after bad? Or, apart from finances, trusting a person with some vital information immediately after previous information has been betrayed? Hardly! Because forgiving means to truly help someone in their need in spite of how they have hurt you. But it is not helping a person if we enable that person to sin again in the same way – or to do

223

anything that will enable sinning. Forgiving means, not merely saying: I forgive you, but to truly help the one who has hurt you so that sometimes saying "no" is the truly helpful thing to do.

A related reminder: forgiving is not forgetting, as even Jesus shows in this text; for how could you have actually forgotten the hurtful sin of an hour or so ago? That truly is impossible! God can forget our sins, but we are not God, so we can't actually forget. But we can act in kindness to help even when we remember the hurt – or still suffer from it. Jesus' continuing to bless us is His forgiving us. He is why, He is how, we can forgive, help in spite of remembering.

Another side of this forgiving process is that we live as kindly as we can so that others don't have to forgive us so often. Of course, because of our human weakness we do need others to forgive us for how we sin against them. It's inevitable, no matter how hard we try not to, still, at times we do hurt others, sometimes unknowingly because we don't think about the effect our actions or our words might have upon others, other times, of course, in anger or in meanness (which results from revengeful anger) we deliberately hurt someone. Or it could be out of selfishness that we act against others. Think of politics as example. "Negative ads" can be merely reporting how one's opponent has failed in one way or another. But usually "negative ads" are those which viciously attack and misinterpret the opponent's deeds or proposals. That is deliberate sin! How many millions of dollars of deliberate sin are we being assaulted with in this political campaign? Unfortunately for our country, there won't be much forgiving after this campaign is over, because most of the campaigners show little evidence of faith in Jesus for their own forgiveness. May none of us be deliberately doing or speaking sin politically.

As for our daily living: may we keep remembering how God forgives us our sinning because of Jesus so that we not only forgive others, but also so we as much as possible keep from sinning against others so as to not need their forgiveness as much – which two go together: living in kindness keeps us from sinning against others, living in kindness is how we truly are forgiving those who sin against us.

October 14, 2012

Theme: **Doing Good**

Related Reading: Matthew 5:13-20

Text: Philippians 2:14-16

LIKE A CANDLE IN THE DARKNESS

Although our text says we are to "shine like stars in the universe", that sounds too glorious for this sinner at least. It is more realistic for me to try to live like a candle in the darkness of this world. For one thing, a star generates its own light, while a candle has to be lighted by someone to give any light. Spiritually, in ourselves we have no power to do anything other than add to the darkness by our sinning. We can do good – be a light in a spiritual sense – only as the Holy Spirit "ignites" us, that is, brings us to faith, and then keeps working in us to show others what God is like by forgiving, since we have been forgiven, and by doing good to help others, since God keeps doing good and helping us in our needs.

Another difference between a star and a candle is, except for distortion due to distance, a star gives a steady light while it is in the nature of a candle to waver and flicker because of the air currents hitting it. And we, no matter how hard we try to "let our light shine" in serving God, we waver because of our sinful nature and because of the pressures and temptations of life around us. Yes, the best I can do is be a candle for our Lord. Same for you, right?

And the "darkness"? Well, a perhaps over-simplified

analysis of the cultures in any nation will explain it, I think. Back in the days of the Roman Empire, for example, there were three basic cultural attitudes: the Stoics, who looked at life almost only from the intellectual point of view with very little emotion; the Epicureans, who wanted to enjoy the "finer things of life": good food, good music, and good romance (meaning, passionate affairs); and then the Bacchanalians, whose primary aim was to live a wild life of wine, women, and violence, because, as the saying goes: "eat, drink , and be merry, for tomorrow we die".

Roman history can almost be divided into three stages, although there were always some of each type in the nation. The Stoic phase would have been the nation-building phase – the thinkers who established and expanded the nation. The Epicurean stage would be the "golden age", when more people aimed to enjoy life and left the fighting to expand or defend the empire to others, including a lot of mercenaries from other nations. And then came the Bacchanalian phase, when most of the people wanted free food and violent entertainment - "bread and circuses (gladiator fights) for the masses" was the governmental motto. That phase destroyed the Roman Empire.

Can you see the parallel process in our country's history, especially these last few decades? Of course, like Rome our nation has had a mixture of these cultural attitudes; but which is now becoming more and more predominant? Obviously, the Bacchanalian! There are still many good solid citizens, willing to work hard and to help others in need. But more and more people just want drink, drugs, entertainment (the more violent the better), and sex – unbridled sex, no matter how perverted. Even the "good" people aren't above getting "high" and having sexual affairs. Even churches more and more give in to the culture of immoral sex – "Christian" entertainers and many pastors having affairs, the divorce rate of church people hardly any different from the general population (according to most surveys), acceptance of sexual perversions and of couples living together before marriage as almost the normal, even for "Christian" young people! God in Scripture calls this "darkness" or as our text terms it: "a crooked and depraved generation".

Yes, truly "depraved"', seen not only regarding homosexual perversion but in the effort by so many to get sex education into younger and younger school grades, because "children are sexual from birth on" (well, sure, physically as male and female, but not actively – unless abused by older perverts). Truly we live in a culture which is more and more becoming "darkness", especially because that so-called sex education provides no morals but approves of any kind of sexual activity.

And we who do trust in Jesus as Savior, are not automatically immune to this darkness. The internet is so handy to tempt us toward darkness as also television cable channels. No wonder our candle "light" flickers.

Still, we do have that "light", the "word of life", our text calls it, which we are to "hold out" so it might "shine" through us into the darkness around us. "The word of life" is the good news that, a., this life is not all there is to life, for there is eternal life instead of eternal darkness and hopelessness, and b., the way to that eternal life has been opened to us, no, better, provided for us through the work of God Himself, come into this world of darkness as Immanuel, God with us, Jesus. We know what He did: lived perfectly, suffered and died under the plan of God. We know why He did it: because we could never be good enough by our efforts – instead we keep adding to the darkness of sin by our sinning. He did everything needed so that anyone – even everyone, except most refuse – can enter that eternal life. We know this – and we trust it is so.

Yet even that trusting is not our accomplishment. For if we use the illustration of a lighthouse showing an ocean swimmer the way to safety, our efforts even to trust would be like that swimmer caught in the riptides of pride, pulling us away from the light. So God has to act, God the Holy Spirit, even to pull us into trusting in Jesus.

Which is, to return to our candle illustration, how our candle is "ignited": the Holy Spirit causes us to trust in Jesus. And then continues to keep our "light" of faith burning, as we keep hearing and remembering that message of what Jesus did and why.

A lighted candle gives light for others to see. Some preachers imply that this happens only as Christians talk to others about Jesus. But no one sees spoken words! Our "candle light" is how we live. So our text says: "Do everything without complaining or arguing so that you may become blameless and pure, children of God without fault" – which means: what God says about how we are to live in thanks for his having given us the "light", faith, is what we are to do without complaint about it being too difficult or arguing about how it would be better if we did things our way. Always be honest! But I might get into trouble if I tell the truth! Always be kind! But that person was just plain mean to me! Always forgive! But he/she hurt me so much! Always be faithful to your spouse! But that person is so attractive! Always show proper respect! But that official is just corrupt and self-serving! Oh, yes, we know how to complain and argue with God's directions for living as He commands, we sure do!

But who knows better: He – or we? And which is better: walking in His way of light – or participating in the ways of darkness? Quite obvious, isn't it? From our own failures we know that our ways are not trustworthy.

So, our effort is to "become blameless and pure, children of God without fault" by trying to obey His way always.

Which, of course, is impossible – which is why we see our candle light of faith wavering instead of flaming pure and straight – which is why we never can get along without remembering the good news of Jesus: He did it all perfectly and suffered for our failures so that God doesn't condemn us as we deserve, as long as we trust in Jesus for the eternal rescue.

With the light of our doing what He tells us to do, we also will "hold out the word of life", we also will tell others, when we can make the opportunity, why we live the way we do. But the living always comes first, otherwise, who will care about words that mean nothing for our living?

Which is why we try to do good to others each day, not only as our duty, but because it has become our way of life as children of God, who have the light of faith in Jesus as our Rescuer.

July 20, 2014

Theme: **Helping Others Physically**

Related Reading: Luke 10:25-37

Text: Hebrews 13:1-3

BROTHER, STRANGER, PRISONER

Some churches teach that our purpose in life as Christians is to glorify God. Unfortunately, that sounds as though if we make sounds of praise with our voices, that fulfills our duty to God. Which is how some people who call themselves "Christian" act: as long as they go to church where God is praised verbally, it doesn't matter much how they live the rest of the week. Such hypocrisy!

Of course, true "praise" involves not merely our tongue, but our entire body as we do what is pleasing to God – that is our real "praise" or "worship" to glorify God. So Paul teaches in Romans 12 (v.1): "Offer your bodies as living sacrifices...which is your spiritual worship" – how we live is how we truly glorify our God and Savior.

Jesus summarizes that way of living with the single word: "love", as He taught the disciples on Maundy Thursday evening: "A new commandment I give you: Love one another. As I have loved you, so you must love one another. All men will know that you are My disciples if you love one another" (John 13:34-35). And John explains that this "love" is not a matter of feeling or of words, but of actually helping others in their physical needs (1 John 3:16-18). So, although we do glorify God through the words of praise we speak or sing, we primarily glorify – give glory or praise to – God by the helping deeds of our lives. Actually, word and deed are two sides of the one "coin" of glorifying God in thanks for how He has helped us for all eternity through Jesus.

Today's text emphasizes how we are to glorify God by how we help three different groups of people: brothers, strangers, prisoners. And as we will see in these three groups, it is hard, harder, and hardest to give the help which each group needs – hard, harder, hardest because of the reluctance of the sinful nature we each have to struggle against.

First group: "Keep on loving each others as brothers". This is the brotherhood of fellow members in one's congregation. Is that hard to do, to love them? Not necessarily, especially at first. But if it wasn't hard, why was the Hebrews author inspired to write: "keep on..."? Because at first, when we come to faith and are so thankful for Jesus – or, when we first enter a congregation and receive a warm welcome (which doesn't always happen, unfortunately, which is why it can be hard to "love each other as brothers"), at first it is a joy to know new people who share faith in Jesus: He rescued me – He rescued you – we praise Him together in worship!

But then we get to know people as they really are, not only on their Sunday best behavior, but as the sinners they also are (and, of course, the reverse is also true that they get to know us as the sinners we are), which makes for hurt feelings at times or self-righteous complaints against some (in our minds anyway); so we don't feel quite as good about some as we did at first. Then combine that with our desire not to get too involved with others, because we have our own lives to live without getting involved in their needs – no wonder it's realistic for the Lord to remind us: "Keep on loving each other as brothers"! Which means: it's not a matter of feeling, but of helping meet the needs of others, which we are to do, because of how Jesus has helped us: suffering and dying for us! So, remember! Help each other in your needs, because Jesus has helped you all in your needs. As John explained (1 John 3:19): "We love, because He first loved us". It should be easy to love – to help – our fellow congregational members. But sometimes our self-centered human natures hinder us. So we have to remember how Jesus has helped us.

Even harder – at least sometimes – is to love, to help, strangers. But our text says: "Do not forget to entertain strangers". Especially in those early years of the Christian church this meant: help fellow Christians who are traveling – show them hospitality – even a bed at night to help them on their way. Not always easy, because who needs this added effort? I've got my own needs to take care of, and these people will upset my schedule! So speaks our sinful nature! And in our day it might add: why spare them a motel bill? Or a meal cost?

Which does not mean that we are to open our table and

our guest bed for just anyone off the street! But we are to be alert to the needs of strangers who come into our lives. Being friendly might open an opportunity to be of real help – even if it costs us time or money. It's hard, however, because too easily we can "pass by on the other side" instead of being a "Good Samaritan".

So it helps us to be reminded: helping the stranger in need is also part of how we glorify God – and our helping is to be because Jesus did not "pass by on the other side" of our world, but came from eternity into our world precisely because we are in utmost need as sinners. But He came – He helped – no, He rescued – He did it all so we could live forever – in blessing. And remembering His help works in us to become willing to help even strangers in need. Still not easy at times, because we do have our own needs with limited time and resources. But if we are remembering, we might be surprised that we can be helpful.

With a possible bonus! For our text adds this little reminder: "for by doing so, some people have entertained angels without knowing it". Some say this refers to Abraham's experience with three strangers (Genesis 18) or Gideon's experience with one stranger (Judges 6); but in both of those experiences the hosts seemed to recognize quickly that these were angels visiting them. Lot, however, as he lived in Sodom (Genesis 19), was hospitable to two strangers and kept them safe from homosexual rape, yet did not realize they were angels until the next day. Not that we will actually "entertain angels", if we help strangers. But it can happen that a friendship relationship might develop, which will give on-going blessings to us and to these new friends. Only the Lord knows in advance what His plan might be when He gives us the opportunity to help a stranger.

And then the hardest situation in which to help – when we might be the most reluctant: to help prisoners. Here God is directing us especially to help fellow Christians who have been imprisoned because of standing up for the faith against government persecution. Which there was plenty of in those early years of the church – with the attendant danger that if a Christian helped an imprisoned Christian, perhaps the government officers would add to the prison population! No wonder there was reluctance! Yet, says our text: "Remember those in prison as if you were their fellow prisoners and those mistreated as if you yourselves were suffering".

Who might this be for us today? Think of Christians right now being persecuted – even killed – in many countries, especially Muslim countries. What can we do? Easy enough to pray for them. But prayer ordinarily requires accompanying action for results to occur. So, might that not mean trying to pressure our government to take actions to work for the human rights of persecuted Christians, such as Christian pastors jailed in Iran and North Korea right now because they won't renounce faith in Jesus? Letters of encouragement sometimes are very helpful also. Demonstrating for justice might also be a way to help – not the mob-frenzy demonstrations which make the news by degenerating into violence, but public protests for real justice.

Jesus said in this connection: "I was in prison and you came to visit Me" (Matthew 25:36). Obviously, He is not referring to those who are justly and unrepentantly imprisoned. However, aren't those prisoners also in need, even in extra need? For if they are not led to repentance and faith in Jesus, their suffering will eventually be far worse than an earthly jail cell. And so, we also should consider ways of helping such prisoners. Which our human nature is reluctant to do, because: "they are getting what they deserve", "they'll only try to scam you", and so on. Not everyone is able to, but maybe the Lord will guide you or me to that opportunity some day.

In all of these calls for us to be helpers to others, we need to remember Jesus, Who has helped us. As we remember that greatest fact each day, He will give us opportunity to help, even when it seems quite difficult. Which is why Paul was inspired to write (Galatians 6:10): "Therefore, as we have opportunity, let us do good to all people, especially to those who belong to the family of believers."

September 28, 2014

Theme: **Helping Others Spiritually**

Related Reading: Luke 15:11-32

Text: James 5:19-20

SPIRITUAL RESUCUE INTERVENTION

The first truth this text teaches is that any Christian, anyone trusting in Jesus now as Savior, could fall away into unbelief – anyone! Some churches teach that "once in faith always in faith", but this text – plus others in the New Testament – absolutely disprove that teaching. Some individuals, perhaps even you, think: Not me! I will never fall away – Jesus means too much to me. But this text says: Wake up! Yes, you! You could! For even St. Paul realized that danger for himself. Read what he says in Philippians 3: "Not that I have already obtained all this or have already been made perfect, but I press on to take hold of that for which Christ Jesus took hold of me" (v.17). Or as he wrote – by inspiration, of course – in 1 Corinthians: "I beat my body and make it my slave so that after I have preached to others, I myself will not be disqualified" (9:27). As long as we have our sinful natures, faith in Jesus is never a "done deal" – anyone could fall away!

For, losing faith can happen so quickly! Not in a mental way (that is, outright saying: I don't believe any longer), but in a physical way. A little innocent flirting with someone can turn into a sexual affair – and that – according to Scripture (Galatians 5, Colossians 3, 1 Thessalonians 4, and more) – is unbelief, a rejection of God's love in Jesus

(1 Thessalonians 4:7), no matter how anyone tries to excuse it.   Murder also – and hatred (1 John 3:15) – refusing to forgive someone (Matthew 6:14) – and the absolutely easiest form of unbelief: self-righteousness: "I'm better than that person"! Anyone of us can fall away from faith – as our text teaches: "if one of you (who now are in faith) should wander from the truth".

And if you see this happening to someone you know who claims to trust in Jesus, what should you do? Just shake your head in sadness?   Or make excuses because it's someone you really care about (a son or daughter perhaps)? Or not try because it's so hard to even broach the subject, since they'll say: None of your business – it's my life – and you're no angel to say anything to me! Because it is so difficult is probably why James writes as he does: "if one should wander...and someone should bring him back" – "if"! Not easy – doesn't always happen even if someone tries!

Still, as Jude wrote: "snatch others from the fire and save them" (v.28) – and Jesus gave specific directions in Matthew 18: "if your brother sins against you...if he listens to you, you have won your brother over" (v.15) with on-going procedures to rescue someone going further and further on the path of unbelief – Jesus requires us to make the effort! His story about the Good Samaritan was directly about helping people in physical need; but we also are not to "pass by on the other side" if it is a matter of spiritual need. Jesus expects us to try!

You have probably heard of what is called an "intervention" with someone whose addiction is harming those close to him or her – it may have to do with alcohol, other drugs, or any compulsion which is harmful. A number of people in that person's life meet with him or her to express their concern and to inform the person about how that behavior is harming those he or she cares about, which often the person does not realize or even remember. "Intervention" isn't easy – and doesn't always work. But it is an effort to try to rescue the afflicted person.

We are called to make spiritual intervention efforts, when a person has denied faith in Christ by their actions, while still claiming faith. As Paul wrote to the Galatians: "Brothers, if someone is caught in a sin, you who are spiritual should restore him gently. But watch yourself or you also may be tempted" (6:1). Obviously Paul is not talking about any and every sin, but about those which deny faith (because Paul writes that the person has to be "restored"), especially because some can spiritually sneak up to "catch" a person so he or she doesn't realize that faith has been denied. Even the instructions Jesus gave in Matthew 18 kind of describe an intervention effort with the aim to rescue, not to get rid of. So, we are called!

But what a difficult responsibility to carry out, partly because of our own sinfulness (we may have been similarly tempted so that "only by the grace of God go I") and partly because of our fear of rejection. Which is why to the Galatians Paul emphasized: "restore him gently" – which means obviously, not with a self-righteous attitude, but with sincere concern for the person's eternal welfare.

Which is also why we have to be acting on the basis of God's clear Word, not just personal feelings. As our text indicates: "whoever turns a sinner away from his error will save him from death", eternal death, as that person comes back to faith. This return to faith would then "cover over" the "multitude of sins", which the person had committed in that time of unbelief, no matter how many or – from our human point of view – how serious. For every sin we or anyone commits has been paid for by the perfect obedience and the suffering and death of Jesus – every sin! Even the atrocities now being committed by the ISIS Muslims, even the spousal abuse and child abuse by pro football players, even that sinning which you and I are still so ashamed of in our past – every single sin – has been covered over – by the blood of Jesus! It's been done!

But, of course, the individuals who have done that sinning aren't personally covered unless they actually trust in what Jesus has done. Also, of course, God says that such trust will stop a person from continuing to do any faith-rejecting sin (more properly called "evil"), so that no one can say: I trust that Jesus died for also my immoral living – but I'm going to keep on living immorally – or holding a grudge so I refuse to forgive – or whatever the evil is. The whole point of God's teaching is: can't have faith while living in these forms of evil – so, you who have by My grace not gotten caught up in evil have this great responsibility to intervene and try to rescue those who have gotten so caught.

We always have to start in and stay in humble, repentant faith ourselves. Only then can we be gentle and sincere. So, daily we are to be sure that we are trusting in Jesus only and not in our own efforts to obey Him, as we live – yet also be sure that we are living His way as much as possible. (This is what Paul meant when he wrote, as I quoted early in this "Message", that he had to "press on to take hold of" what Jesus had called him to, eternal life – faith always requires the effort to be faithful.)

Which happens only as we keep in mind day by day the message of the Gospel: I obeyed and suffered for all your sinning, even that sinning you haven't done yet – it all is covered over by My blood – as you trust only in My completed work for you. That message is what keeps us in faith so that we can try to rescue others from the trap of unbelief which still has them "caught".

So, whom do you care about who is so "caught"? And what can you do to "intervene", to talk to that person who has left faith for unbelieving living? Although "intervention" works best when more than just one are involved, still, in most spiritual situations it has to begin and usually continue with just one person. Which is implied, at least, in our text: "*someone* should bring him back" and "*whoever* turns the sinner away", both in the singular. Sometimes a group of Christians will be involved, but even the group begins with just one.

So easily in our day Christians can get "caught" by impulsive evil so that faith is thrown away, often without the person realizing it at first. Such is the danger also for ourselves. And such is why the Lord calls us to gently and humbly try to rescue those who are now "caught".

October 5, 2014

Theme: **Judging Others**

Related Reading: Matthew 7:13-23

Text: James 4:11-12

BUT WE HAVE TO JUDGE!

This whole matter of not judging others is at least somewhat confusing, it seems to me. Our text says: "Who are you to judge your neighbor?" Jesus in the Sermon on the Mount said (Matthew 7:1): "Do not judge or you too will be judged". And yet Jesus judged others – He judged the disciples ("You of little faith, why are you so afraid?" – Matthew 8:26 – on the stormy Sea of Galilee), and He often judged the Pharisees. And we can't explain this by thinking: Well, He is God, so He had the right to judge – because He was speaking as a man in human situations.

We are also told to "judge" others in the sense of warning them, when they are sinning – Paul even condemns the immoral couple in 1 Corinthians 5. Also, even in the Sermon on the Mount shortly after saying we are not to "judge", Jesus says we must judge "false prophets" (7:15, 20) we are to judge whether a person is teaching what God says or just his own ideas – you are to judge even this "Message" in that way to be sure I do not mislead you. So, you see what I mean that this matter of "not judging" is "at least somewhat confusing"? Enough so that perhaps you have had a friend or a family member retort, when you pointed out their obvious sinning: "Who are you to judge me?"

So, what's the explanation? Our text says: "Who are you to judge your neighbor?", but we have to judge, don't we, at least at times? When is judging wrong and when is it required?

The answer lies in the definition of "judging". Jesus somewhat explained this when He told the unbelieving Jews: "Do not think I will accuse you before the Father. Your accuser is Moses" (John 5:45), meaning: it is the written Word of God which judges. Which means: if we are applying only God's Word in our warning someone of their sinning, then we are not "judging", but He is.

However, even then it depends on how we use God's Word in warning someone else. If we arrogantly just condemn as though we are so good and the other person is so bad, then we are judging. Instead, as Jesus taught (Matthew 7:5 – Sermon on the Mount again): first we have to admit our own sinning and remember our being forgiven so that we can speak to someone else humbly with the aim of getting that person to accept forgiveness so he/she can change to do right instead of wrong. But it is "judging" if all we are actually interested in is condemning that person to try to make them feel bad enough to stop – or just to make that person feel bad, period! In short, if our aim is to hurt instead of to help, then we are judging.

Also we are judging if we find fault not because the person is doing wrong according to what God says, but because that person is not meeting our standards, our desires. Such as, to use myself as example: I personally do not like tattoos – of course, I have a right to my opinion, but if (although sometimes it is "when") I even think less of a person who has tattoos, then I am judging, setting myself up as better because that person does not meet my personal taste.

We all do this to a certain extent in a variety of ways, dependent on how strong our personal tastes are: a rabid Yankee fan can hardly stand a Red Sox fan – someone who loves classical music considers him/herself more intelligent than a rock music enthusiast. And then there is prejudice, racial or nationality prejudice: Norwegians and Swedes famously have not gotten along with each other – so many whites don't think blacks are very intelligent, while so many blacks automatically suspect whites of being racists (which is also a form of racism). Racism, of course, is not a harmless prejudice – prejudice is sin – James 2 clearly teaches this (using the prejudice of someone better off vs. poor). And all "judging" in its actual sense of wanting to hurt or despising on the basis of personal opinion – is sin according to our text and the other places Scripture says "don't judge"!

What compounds this sin of judging, however – and this is the special point of this text – is to speak badly of others on the basis of one's judging: "Do not slander one another. Anyone who speaks against his brother or judges him, speaks against the law and judges it." "Slander" would be speaking outright falsehood, while "judging" is speaking against others, as I've mentioned already, on the basis of personal preference which goes beyond what God's Law says. It's bad enough to personally think badly of others, but to speak those thoughts publicly means we have increased our guilt. By how much? By in essence announcing that God didn't know what He was doing when He gave only the commands which He did, but did not include what we think is wrong: we are setting ourselves up over God, when we sinfully judge on the basis of more than what He clearly teaches in His Word. And who are we to judge God?

Especially in view of how serious this is, how blessed we are that He Who truly is the "Judge" is "the One Who is able to save" as well as destroy. He should destroy us, that is, punish us forever. He has every right to pass such a sentence upon each of us, not only because of our sinful judging, but also because of all our other sinning, all those times – and it happens daily to a greater or lesser degree – that we know what He has commanded, both what to do and what not to do, yet we disobey, doing what we want to do instead of what He says. He says "Don't" – and we do it anyway – sometimes reluctantly (I mean, we know it's wrong to listen to bad gossip, for example, the talk about the wrong things others have done just as casual conversation, but we usually don't try to stop someone else from speaking that slander, not only because we are afraid because of what others might say if we try, but also because our sinful nature wants to use that knowledge about someone else's sinning to increase our self-righteous thinking that "I guess I'm not so bad after all"). But usually we do the "don't"s very willingly, because that's what we want! Yes, we deserve Your punishment even to destroy us, heavenly Judge. Also because so often what You command us to do, we don't do – for our own reasons; example, we don't always help others in need because we can't be bothered or don't want to use our time or money that way. Guilty again, oh Judge! I deserve whatever punishment You decide is just.

But in admitting that, we are not despairing. For we know our heavenly Judge as the One Who also can save instead of destroy. And so has He decided and acted. That's what the "good news" of Jesus is all about: to save! That's what the very name "Jesus" actually means; as Joseph was told: "You are to give Him the name Jesus, because He will save His people from their sins" (Matthew 1:21) – the strict translation of "Jesus" from both the Greek and the Hebrew is: God saves.

How? We know: He not only died for us, He also lived for us – He didn't do the "don't"s – He did the "do"s – perfectly. He took our place and survived what would have been destruction for us. So has He saved us.

Or rather, made it possible for us to be saved – as well as every other sinner. The work is all completed! It just has to be applied to us! Which is what we call "faith", trusting that by what He did, we are saved from eternal destruction. When we are convinced by this "good news" message, then we are saved – we receive what He accomplished – which "faith" is always a "work in progress", however, meaning: it is a daily trusting, trusting in Him alone, not trusting that we are good enough (at least better than someone else). Instead: "By grace (God's love carried out in Jesus) you have been saved through faith – and this not from yourselves, it is the gift of God – not by works, so that no one can boast" (Ephesians 2:8-9).

Which does not stop right there! For the next verse of Paul's sentence is: "We are God's workmanship, created (He has made us into new creatures with a spiritual nature in contrast to only our inherited sinful nature) in Christ Jesus to do good works" (v.10). Faith gives us ability and desire to do the good and right things as God, the Law-giver, has commanded.

Among which commands are these about judging. We are to "judge" in the sense of recognizing sin – first in ourselves and only then in others – so that we can speak about forgiveness being needed and being available for anyone, no matter what the sinning is. We can't be nit-picking fault-finders, for that is just plain judging, meaning, condemning. But we encourage each other, warning each other when necessary and when appropriate (when we have private opportunity); we speak of forgiveness so that the other person will have the spiritual strength to try to do different, as we keep trying to do in our own lives.

Lord, help us to be humble and kind helpers for our fellow sinners – because You have forgiveness for all of us.

Theme: **Hypocrisy**

Related Reading: James 2:1-13

Text: Isaiah 1:10-20

NO COVERUP BEFORE GOD

Almost always when I think about hypocrites in congregations, I remember how more than one non-church-going North Dakota farmer said as excuse: Your congregation has so many hypocrites, like the grain elevator manager. I would smile in sadness for that unbeliever, because in the five North Dakota congregations I served only one had a member who was a grain elevator manager and I had heard only good about Gene Ellingrud.

Which is not to say that congregations don't have some member hypocrites, men – or women – who attend regularly, but who live daily as though they hadn't attended at all! Such individuals apparently think that they can cover up their evil living by a show of public worship. If I became aware of such a contradiction, I tried as a pastor to help that person turn from unbelief to actual faith. But a hypocrite by definition is not too obvious most of the time so a pastor usually doesn't know. Then, too, there is the hypocrisy which says "I trust in Jesus as Savior" but which actually depends on one's own "good deeds", whether that is attending public worship or doing good things. Outward action does not cover up inner lack of faith before God, although humans can be fooled.

Sometimes, of course, hypocrisy gets very publicly exposed. How many pastors or others have had their unbelief shown by revelations about sexual affairs, even homosexual relationships, or about financial corruption or by promoting beliefs which completely contradict the essential Christian faith – such as denying Jesus' physical resurrection or teaching that the Muslim "god" is actually the same as the true God, the Triune God! Such individuals had tried to cover up their unbelief by great shows of religiosity, of religious ritual. But there is no coverup before God for them! God sees the reality of their actual beliefs, not just the show they put on. And sometimes other people also find out.

Such was the situation Isaiah was condemning in our text. The leaders and the people, most of them, were performing religious rituals, but they were not trying at all to live God's way in daily life. It's interesting to notice how Isaiah addresses them: "You rulers of Sodom...you people of Gomorrah." But these two city-kingdoms had been destroyed more than a 1000 years before Isaiah lived! Yet the evil of those two cities – and the evil was homosexual living – was so despicable that those names were still used to condemn any nation which lived so blatantly contrary to God's way, while pretending to be so good before God by being so regular in religious ritual: public outward form but daily evil living!

It is interesting also how God condemns their public religious practices by asking: Who told you to do these things – sacrifices, offerings, incense, festivals, even prayer? But, Lord! You told us to do them! Not if they were merely meaningless forms, duties to perform so you can keep on with evil living! Sacrifices especially are to mean: I'm sorry – forgive me – I don't want to do that sin again! But you! You kill people – you do evil – you practice wrong – you take advantage of helpless, needy people! Because you live so evil, "I will hide My eyes from you" no matter how much you pray and give sacrifices! You cannot cover up your life of unbelief with a pretense of religious forms! You can't fool Me! And so God condemns hypocrisy, pretending to believe!

Which condemnation should also make us uncomfortable before God! For don't we all have some hypocrisy in our lives? You don't want other people to know some of what you've done – or still do – or how you sometimes think, do you? I don't!

However, there is a difference here, a difference between an outright pretending coverup and our own failings. Not to excuse ourselves, for we are guilty – we all are guilty of not living up to the faith we profess – for, remember: faith is not merely a matter of proper words in our heads and through our lips; faith shows itself in daily living – or it isn't faith at all! Not that there ever is perfection in our lives – there always is the struggle to do what is right, what is good. But if we have the attitude that it doesn't matter how we sin and that we fail, that is not faith but unbelief. And that can't be covered up before God by prayer or church work or church attendance. That's what the people of Judea were doing, which God through Isaiah condemns in our text.

The way of faith is for us in our failures to come to the Lord for the comfort of forgiveness and – which is the essential addition – and His help to do different, to struggle to do right instead of wrong, good instead of bad. It's called repentance: turning from sin, the devil's way, and turning to God's way, through the power of God's forgiveness working in us to give us peace for the past and power for the future. We come to God with the desire that our failures – which we don't want others even to know about, but which He knows – that our failures might be struggled against and overcome more and more.

This is what God in our text is talking about when Isaiah quotes Him as saying: "Come now, let us reason together; though your sins are like scarlet, they shall be as white as snow; though they are red as crimson, they shall be like wool." God wants to forgive! And to change! Us! The two actions going together: forgiveness and change! Which does not happen merely by God saying "forgiveness" all by itself. When God says "let us reason together", He is actually saying: You need to think with Me about how I am able to forgive you. My reasoning is that I will use My Son, come to earth as the perfect Sacrifice for your sins. Your animal sacrifices – God was saying to these Old Testament people – really are nothing in themselves, but are really foreshadowings, prophecies, of what I will do in His sacrifice. Because of Him I can forgive you – as you trust in what He would do, I do forgive you.

But! If you won't accept My reasoning and instead insist on your way of coverup thinking and continued evil living – "if you resist and rebel, you will be devoured by the sword." Which is what happened to those Old Testament people! They received no forgiveness, and they suffered in this life as well as forever!

We, who live now, know that God did carry out His "reasoning", His plan. It took centuries, but finally God did send His Son, "He gave His one and only Son", gave Him into perfect living, into being the sacrifice for sin, all sin, so "that whoever believes in Him shall not perish but have eternal life" (John 3:16) because of being forgiven in this life. That's God's "reasoning" – Jesus is His plan – and by faith in Jesus we are forgiven! So that we can also change – to be more of how He plans for us to live.

Which is why we come to worship sincerely. We come, not to "cover up", but because we know we can't hide from God. So we come – to be assured: forgiven! And to be encouraged: Yes, I will help you in your struggle to live My way day by day.

February 24, 2013

Theme: **Hear and Do**

Related reading: Matthew 7:13-29

Text: 1 Corinthians 6:9-11

EASIER SAID THAN DONE

Could anything be more clear? God in our text very emphatically says: "The wicked will not inherit the kingdom of God"! And who are "the wicked"? The next verse specifies exactly whom He means – and He adds the warning: "Do not be deceived" – by human reasoning or excuses – no! "Neither the sexually immoral nor adulterers nor male prostitutes nor homosexual offenders nor thieves nor the greedy nor drunkards nor slanderers nor swindlers will inherit the kingdom of God"! Which means that, even though surveys show that over half of all Americans claim to be "born-again Christians", most Americans "will not inherit the kingdom of God", but will go to hell instead of heaven!

And why can that judgment be made? Because how obvious it is that Americans on the whole are caught up in sexual immorality and/or drunkenness (not only from alcohol but by other drugs – no difference) – which is only getting worse with the legalization of "recreational marijuana" to "get high" (which is drunkenness). Think also of the whole "college experience" of so many, not attending to truly learn, but to "party", meaning drunkenness and sex. Also, "greedy"? How about politicians who receive large salaries with many benefits, yet vote themselves to have more? Same with public sector unions whose members are never satisfied no matter that they bankrupt their communities (not all do, of course, but there are many examples which prove this). But then it's also greed for our general population to want more and more and more things! And "swindlers"? So much false advertising – even with claims that are absolutely not true!

Nor are church members immune from this judgment, not when statistics show that the rate of divorce – which primarily involves sexual immorality – is little different among churched people than among the unchurched. And many clergy are included as so many have to admit to sexual affairs or are practicing homosexuals or addicted to pornography or are sexual child abusers. And "greedy"? Clergy not immune to this wickedness either – especially the bureaucrats who aren't involved in day-to-day spiritual work with members of a congregation, but who receive outrageous salaries and still want more! And so many everyday pastors also expecting increased annual salaries! Then there is the whole area of slander, gossip about the sins – or supposed sins – of others – especially celebrities! What a flourishing industry that is in our country! In view of these facts one has to judge on the basis of God's plain Word that most Americans are "wicked" and "will not inherit the kingdom of God".

Not that anyone admits to being – or thinks of him or her self as "wicked"! Those practicing homosexuality claim they are only living as they were "made" and will charge a person with "hate speech" for calling them "wicked" no matter if God's Word is being quoted about being "wicked". And those who engage in heterosexual immorality? Well, just doing what is natural – and, if one should admit it isn't what God's Word says, then: but it's only a sin and all sins are forgiven, aren't they?, so don't call me "wicked"! Even a prostitute might say: I'm only making a living – so I'm not "wicked" – in fact, I'm even providing a service to men! And on and on come the excuses and the reasoning! But God clearly says here: "Do not be deceived! The wicked will not inherit the kingdom of God!" And in this text He doesn't even mention the wickedness of murder and hate (1 John 3:15) and refusing to forgive (Matthew 6:15).

God caused Paul to write this clear condemnation to the Corinthian congregation, not so they would pride themselves like the Pharisee in the temple who said: "I thank You that I am not like other men – robbers, evildoers, adulterers" (Luke 18:11), but as a warning: you once did these things – and you are still tempted to do them – in fact, in the previous chapter Paul had condemned them for allowing a man to remain a member even though he was guilty of "sexual immorality...of a kind that does not occur even among pagans" (5:1). And so also Christians are warned: Be on guard! It would be so easy for you to fall into that way of living: immorality, drunkenness, greed, idolatry even.

By the way, why does God here emphasize sexual sinning (four of the ten forms of wickedness are sex-related – and let's realize that in God's judgment homosexual immorality is no worse than heterosexual immorality – both are equally "wicked")? Why? Because sex is so easily a temptation, not only because lust is so much a part of our sinful nature, but also because the example and the opportunity are so much around us. So, Christians, be on your guard!

Which also is God's warning to you personally, if you should be involved in any of these wicked ways of living! Face up to it! God says it is wickedness and will not be allowed by Him in His people. Do you hear Him? Will you do what He says – or what your sinful nature wants and what so many around you claim to be enjoying? Will you hear and do and be blessed? Or will you keep turning away from Him to your wicked ways? Surely you don't want to continue outside of His kingdom, do you?

Easier said than done, however – to change, that is, to turn away from wickedness which you've been involved in – and find some kind of satisfaction in. I mean, sex gives a person a thrill – drunkenness gives an escape (temporary though it is) – greed gives the pride of "mine" – and so on. Not at all easy to quit evil to do good! Which is true also if you are not involved in wickedness – which, I pray, most of you are not so involved. But each of us has sin which we know we should turn away from. Perhaps it is the short leash we have on our temper – or the tendency to "stretch" the facts of a situation to always make ourselves look better than others. Or selfishness with time or effort or money. Or just plain laziness which leads us to do other things – or nothing at all – instead of using our time wisely and helpfully. And … what is there in your life that shouldn't be – because God says it is wrong, but still is there – and has been for a long time? What do you need to change? As I know things that I need to change in my life. Perhaps you can join me in saying: but I'm working at changing at least – I'm trying!

Easier said than done, however, right? Easier wanted than accomplished! And the more serious the sin – when it falls into the "wickedness" category, the harder it is. Ask any alcoholic – or perhaps you know that by the experience of having worked to escape any wickedness, whether an addiction or sexual sinning or whatever. Easier said than done – no matter how much we want to change.

Yet, it can be done! Paul writes: "That is what some of you WERE"! Some of those Corinthian Christians had lived in such wickedness! But not any more! Some had changed – even though they were still tempted, as Paul here is warning them. So if some had changed (and still today some have changed from drug addiction, alcohol or harder – from homosexual participation – from sexual affairs – from a life of crime – from hating others), if even in our day some have changed, others can also – even though "easier said than done".

How? By the power of God's good news of forgiveness in Jesus! Which Paul immediately writes about – as a reminder against recurring temptation – and as on-going power to do what God commands. He wrote: "But you were washed, you were sanctified, you were justified in the name of the Lord Jesus Christ and by the Spirit of our God". When you came to faith in Jesus by hearing the message that Jesus paid even for your most detestable wickedness as well as for all your other – by comparison – less serious sinning (although just one sin would destroy the holiness we need to enter the eternal kingdom of God – yet humanly we can see – as God does in these verses – the more in contrast to the less serious), that He took them all on Himself and endured the "outside the kingdom" consequences of them so that, as you came to trust in Jesus to so take your place, you have been "washed" by His blood so that you are now "clean", that is, holy in God's sight – "sanctified" says our text – because He has "justified" you, that is, declared you innocent – not because you are innocent, but because of Jesus: "in the name of the Lord Jesus Christ" in Whom you have faith "by the Spirit of our God". So, having been washed clean by the work of Jesus, you have been freed from the power of that sin with its temptations. You don't have to any more – you can live as God says instead.

This is the power God gives us in His message of Jesus as Savior to face and fight and overcome any temptation to wickedness and any sin. His power is strong enough to help us leave every kind of wickedness – anyone can – as some in that Corinthian congregation did – and others since then have; takes much effort, much being encouraged and strengthened by that message, but it can be done!

It would seem that the same powerful message should be able to free us from every form of sinning also. And in theory it can! But because we will always have our sinful nature until we finally enter "the (eternal) kingdom of God", we never can overcome every single form of sinning. We work at it – we try, but at the end of each day we still have to confess: Lord, be merciful to me, sinner that I am.

And so we are comforted – that we are forgiven. Which makes us determined to keep turning away from what God says is wrong to doing what He says is good and right. As we do keep hearing the good He wants us to do along with the good He has done for us in Jesus, we are able to do the good He commands more and more so that we don't have as much time to think as much of the sin He has freed us from, even though we still are tempted at times by it.

It's all "easier said than done" – but can be done – by His powerful help!

August 17, 2014

Theme: **Fearful**

Related Reading: Matthew 14:22-33

Text: Isaiah 42:1-9

HE HOLDS OUR HAND

Why do couples hold hands when walking – or even just sitting? Ahh, when love is passionate, there just has to be touching. But why when love is settled and mature, why do even some older couples still hold hands? Isn't it because it means: "I care about you"? And even more, doesn't it mean: "And I will care for you – I am here to help you"? And isn't there a similar meaning if you hold the hand of someone who is hurting – or dying? I'm here – I care about you – I'll help you however I can.

Holding another person's hand is more meaningful, it seems to me, than a hug. For a hug is fleeting – and can be merely a social custom. But to hold a person's hand means: I do care about you.

That's what God means when He says in our text through Isaiah: "I will take hold of your hand." I will help You do what You need to do for My wandering children. For, you see, these verses are primarily meant for Jesus, "My servant" (v.1), the Lord calls Him, the One Who would be "a covenant with the people", meaning His people Israel, but also extending to the Gentiles (v.6). God is promising this to Jesus according to His human nature, which knew how difficult, how painful it would be to establish   that "covenant", the covenant of forgiveness through faith. That's why Jesus prayed as He did in the Garden of Gethsemane: if possible, Father, if there can be any other way, let Me avoid all this pain – yet: "not My will but Yours be done" (Luke 22:42). So, already in the Old Testament God the Father is promising: I will be there to help You do what must be done to rescue all My lost children!

However, although this promise was directed specifically for "My servant", Jesus, it also applies to and comforts us, who now are in that covenant which He established. For He cares about us, even though we so often show that we don't always care about Him. I mean, what else are our sins but a not caring about Him enough so we insist on our way instead of His way in living. His caring for us is why He sent His servant, Jesus, in the first place. He loved – and loves – us so He sent Jesus for us. And even though our caring for Him, which is another way of describing our faith, our trust in what He has done through Jesus, is very weak at times – or perhaps even usually – though our faith is like "a bruised reed" or a "smoldering wick", He cares so much that He will not "break" it or "snuff (it) out", but will use His power to keep us His – and also to build up our caring so the "reed" of our faith is stronger, so the "wick" of our trust is burning brighter. This is part of the promise He gives us by "tak(ing) hold of our hand".

Of course, this doesn't happen just automatically without our involvement. God cannot use His power in us if we aren't where His power can reach us. Sure, God could just force us! He Who has the power to have created the universe and has the power to give people the breath of life, He could just overpower us, force us! But He doesn't! He appeals to us instead! His Word shows that His power comes to us not through what He has created, but through what He says about what He has done by "His servant". It is only as we hear that "speaking" which He caused to be written down so all people could receive it, only through the explanation and application of that Word through preaching and Bible reading can He work His power in us. If we don't come to where He has His message proclaimed, explained, and applied, His power will not help us. To a certain extent, if we just come to His written Word by our own reading, He can work in us. But He has commanded that we come together with others to receive His message, His assurance, His help for our faith, our caring for Him. That's how He more easily strengthens the "reed" of our faith, the "wick"of our caring.

Yet He also wants to assure us that He cares for us and will help us as we face the troubles of life, the fears that come into us. That's really what He wants us to know as He holds our hand. The struggle of faith is one thing – and I help you in that by the power of My message; but the fears in life are another thing. And I want you to know that I will always use My power to help you when those fears attack. For think of My almighty power! I used it to create the heavens and the earth. I used it to give life also to you. I am still using My power to help you in living. What you can be confident of is how I use My power also to control what happens to you as you live. I do not promise that troubles, that fearful things, will never happen. Sin is behind all of that – trouble and fearful things happen as a result of sin, sometimes as a result of how you have sinned with the consequences being stressful, but usually because of the sinning of others. I cannot eliminate sin in this world – I will in the new creation, but in this creation sin is inevitable. And the consequences can be so fearful as to make you wonder what will happen to me now?

Same also regarding sickness. If there had never been sin, there would never be sickness or death. But sin has weakened our bodies just in general so that illness results – and finally death. And these fears can erupt in our minds: am I going to die of this illness? How painful will it be? But, My child, says our Lord: I'm holding your hand – I'll help you endure it – I will take you through this – I will finally take you home to be with Me forever; for, remember, that's what My servant, Jesus, has established in the "new covenant" of His blood: He shed His blood for you – He suffered everything for you – so you can have peace and blessing forever instead. You don't have to worry or fret – I've got hold of your hand – I'm here and will help you.

Which is His assurance for us when any kind of fear attacks, when any kind of danger threatens. I've got hold of your hand – I care – I will help you – I will take care of you in this life, as I have taken care of you for eternal life.

Which is why we can relax no matter what we face. To be sure, we don't always! At times we let fear and worry dominate our thinking. Especially then we need to come to His proclaimed promises, to hear again: He holds our hand – He will help. And also we need to come to actually feel His touch, that is, the touch of the very Body and Blood of His servant Jesus, in Holy Communion. For that truly is His touch, His very personal, specific touch: "given and shed for you"!

So, perhaps at least from time to time, as you hold hands with someone you care about, you can also think: And He holds my hand and will be working always to help me.

March 3, 2013

Theme: **Suffering**

Related Reading: Matthew 5:1-12

Text: Job 2:1-6

THE LIMITS OF SUFFERING

Don't you have to feel sorry for poor old Job? Although he wasn't poor to begin with: 10 adult children, 7000 sheep, 7000 camels, 1000 oxen, 500 donkeys "and a large number of servants" (1:2-3). Nor was he very old, since, when all was said and done, he was young enough to father ten more children and live to see his great-great-grandchildren (42:12-17). BUT! Think of what happened to him: all his animals were rustled or killed, all his servants were killed by marauders or natural disaster – all except four, and all his children were killed by a windstorm, all this on the same day! All he had left were four servants, a wife who was crazed by grief, and his health. Could anything worse happen to him?

Yes! Next Job lost his health, being afflicted with sores from head to foot, perhaps a kind of psoriasis! And his wife sneered at his faith! And then three friends came – to "sympathize and comfort him" (2:11), they said; but they ended up accusing him of having done something very wrong to deserve this suffering. Great friends, right? Especially since Job had been as good a person as humanly possible ("This man was blameless and upright; he feared God and shunned evil" – 1:1). But these "friends" in effect said: what kind of secret evil have you been hiding? Repent of it! No sympathy! Accusation instead! Could it get any worse for Job?

And the answer now is: No! Job had reached the limits of his suffering. For all that happened was not God's punishment, but God's testing as He allowed the devil to attack Job to try to destroy his faith. At first the Lord had set the limits of his suffering at the loss of everything he had (1:12). When that didn't work for the devil, because Job remained faithful and accepting: "The Lord gave and the Lord has taken away; blessed be the name of the Lord" (1:21), so, when that first attack didn't work for the devil's plan, the Lord allowed the devil to attack Job's person, his health. But that was the limit! "He is in your hands; but you must spare his life" (2:6). The limits of Job's suffering had been set by the Lord, and the devil could go no further!

Now actually, the devil did succeed – almost. For Job did finally start to complain against God, in effect saying: How could You? I don't deserve this! Which means that Job's sinful nature did show itself. But Job never turned completely away from the Lord. And when the Lord reprimanded him, Job repented: "I despise myself and repent in dust and ashes" (42:6). And the Lord forgave him and restored him to health, wealth, and family.

Why? Why did the Lord forgive Job and restore blessings to him? Not because he had a clear faith in Jesus as Savior – no one in the Old Testament had that word-by-word faith. However, Job did have faith in a "Redeemer", as he had confessed: "I know that my Redeemer lives, and that in the end He will stand on the earth. And after my skin has been destroyed, yet in my flesh I will see God, I myself will see Him with my own eyes – I, and not another" (19:25-27). So Job depended, not on his own goodness or efforts, but on Someone Who would "redeem" him, buy him free from his sinfulness. Job did not know Jesus by name, but he trusted that somehow Someone would rescue him from the punishment which he did deserve. And when he did waver with a self-pitying "I don't deserve this", he was forgiven for that sinning because of the Redeemer to come.

Why did all this happen to Job? As God reveals in Romans: "Everything that was written in the past was written to teach us, so that through endurance and the encouragement of the Scriptures we might have hope" (15:4). For, although most likely we will never suffer as much as Job did, still at times we might feel as devastated as Job finally did: one thing after another and another – can it get any worse? And then more comes until we wonder: is there no end? I can't take it any more!

But Job's experience teaches us that although God allows, He always does set limits on what He permits the devil to plot and do against us. What happens to us who trust in Jesus as Savior never is punishment from God. God has already punished Jesus for all our sins. If a person does not trust in Jesus, then God does punish that sinner. And, of course, sometimes God allows the consequences of sin to afflict also a Christian, a truster in Jesus. This is referred to in

Hebrews 12, which says that "the Lord disciplines those He loves, and He punishes everyone He accepts as a son [His child]" (v.6) – which means that if a Christian leaves faith temporarily, such as to get drunk or to live immorally, the Lord will allow consequences, even send them, in order, if possible, to bring that wandering child back to Him in repentant faith. Of course, if that spiritual wanderer insists on continuing in that evil way of life, God will punish – forever (Galatians 5:21 clearly says: "I warn you, as I did before, those who live like this will not inherit the kingdom of God"). But for sin which is not a denial of faith, God does not punish the sinner who trusts in Jesus, for He was punished for our sins.

Actually, Jesus was punished even for the evils people do, that drunkenness, that immorality, all evil – that's why there is forgiveness available for every human being. No one has to suffer for any sin or evil they have done. But if there is no faith in Jesus, then people are punished for their unbelief – eternally.

But to learn further from Job's experience: no punishment from God, but all suffering is inflicted upon us by the devil, who is the source of all the hurt and evil which assault us. Also, the Lord always sets limits on how much the devil can do so that it will never be more than we can endure, as we rely on Him for His help ("God is faithful; He will not let you be tempted beyond what you can bear" – 1 Corinthians 10:13 – this verse says "tempted", but suffering always is also temptation, the temptation to get self-righteous: "I don't deserve this" – or to rebel against God: "Why should I trust You, God, when You allow this to happen to me?") So: suffering is not punishment and God sets limits to suffering so that we can endure it.

But why does God even allow suffering? To a certain extent He cannot in this life shield us from all the effects and consequences of sin, especially sin by others. People sin, verbally, violently, unthinkingly – and others suffer, we suffer. Also, sickness comes, because our bodies have been weakened by the effects of the sinful nature. Suffering is a part of human life, no escaping it completely – because of sin. Why some individuals suffer so much more than others, that we can never know. But when we are suffering – to whatever degree, we can be comforted in knowing that God sets limits so that it will never get to be too much for us. Instead, it will drive us to ask His help to endure it.

Which is one of the reasons why God allows suffering. Too easily we think that we can manage by ourselves; being attacked by suffering makes us realize: I can't control everything – I can't manage just on my own – I need help – I need His help. So does the Lord draw us closer to Him, for where else can we go for help? Friends may try, but even the best-intentioned friends may help somewhat yet so easily can say something that makes us feel worse. And pain-relieving or stress-reducing drugs may also help for a while, but can also cause dependency problems. And when the suffering which produces worrying just goes on and on, there is no human help. But the Lord helps us endure, as

He comforts us: I've set limits to your suffering – and I will help you through it all.

Sometimes the Lord also uses the devil's plan as a tool to work good for others through our suffering. Job's example teaching us is one example with the best example being the suffering of Jesus. The devil planned to get Him killed in order to end His mission – that's what the devil in his short-sighted vision thought. But look how God used that suffering to benefit us! In much smaller ways He might use how we endure suffering to encourage and help others. Which possibility is good to know and, therefore, might help us to endure, although it doesn't lessen our suffering.

Suffering is unavoidable. Yet, when we suffer, we can be confident that we are in our Lord's loving hands and that He has set limits to our suffering so it will never become too much for us. And we also can be comforted in knowing that finally, if our suffering does not end in this life, at last He will take us to the relief and peace and joy of eternal life, not because we suffered, but because Jesus, the Redeemer, suffered for us.

July 14, 2013

Theme: **Tragedy**

Related Reading: Matthew 8:23-27

Text: Acts 27:21-26

WILL YOU SURVIVE CATASTROPHE?

What a storm they are experiencing in the eastern half of the nation! Not a catastrophe like Hurricane Sandy, but mighty serious.

And what a storm St. Paul experienced in our text. Not a catastrophe, although it would have been if the ship and passengers had all been lost. As it turned out, only the ship and cargo were lost.

Which could have been avoided – if the captain had only listened to Paul. But he and the others in command in effect said: what does a land lubber know about sea weather – especially just a Jewish teacher? So, although the sailing season was about over and because the port they were in was "unsuitable to winter in, the majority decided to sail on, hoping to reach" a better harbor further along the coast of Crete (27:12).

And the weather seemed to cooperate! "A gentle south wind began to blow" (v.13), so they sailed out. Right into "a wind of hurricane force, called the 'Northeaster'" (v.14) – which name happens to be almost exactly what New Englanders call storms which blast in from the northeast with vicious winds and rain – "Nor'easter" is the name they give to that type of storm, if I remember correctly from my year of vicarage (practical training with a congregation) there.

The ship was quickly in trouble – and the sailors knew it! They threw the cargo and even the ship's tackle overboard to lighten the ship so it could float more easily as the winds drove it. By the third day, however, they "gave up all hope of being saved" (v.20).

That's when Paul called them all together. He couldn't resist a little "I told you so", but then he encouraged them: Buck up, boys – have courage – an angel of God told me last night that no one would drown. "So keep up your courage men, for I have faith in God that it will happen just as He told me" (v.25).

However, it sure got worse before it got better! According to the verses after our text they had another eleven days of terror before the ship ran aground on the island of Malta. And, just as God had promised, every single one of them, all 276 of those on board, survived! God kept them safe in that near catastrophe.

Catastrophes are a part of normal world history, whether they be natural ones such as earthquake, massive volcanic explosion, hurricane, tornado, or whatever. But catastrophes can also be man-made, that is, due to human evil – such as starvation and massive killing in wartime – or due to human incompetence – such as inferno forest fires because of restrictions set by extreme environmentalists to prevent even sound and sustainable logging practices – or the example of a town built on a historical flood plain, which hadn't flooded in human memory, but which did when massive rains came and literally washed much of the town away! Catastrophes happen! Will you survive, if you are thrown into one?

Maybe yes, maybe no – no one can predict. Even if one takes precautions against possible catastrophes! Such as out here along the Oregon coast, where officials the past couple of years have been warning against a likely Cascadia fault earthquake which could trigger a massive tsunami which would not only destroy all the buildings on the tsunami flood plain (which has been graphically mapped to warn all coastal residents – by the way, our house is high enough in elevation to be safe – but only by a couple of blocks), but which would also disrupt and isolate all the towns along the Oregon coast, because what the tsunami didn't wash away, the effects of the massive earthquake would destroy. And "it's coming" screech governmental officials (and other almost panicky residents) – "the historical average says it's overdue – so it could be any day!" Except the historical average is not the minimum on record, but about 100 years more! However, that catastrophe could happen any day!

Just like any cataclysmic catastrophes could happen to involve you wherever you live. Just about everyone lives near a massive earthquake fault line (a friend told me that even Indiana is in danger) – and if one of our dormant northwest volcanoes suddenly erupts, as St. Helen's did some 30 years ago, or especially if the seething thermal activity under Yellowstone Park should explode, as some seismologists are warning is soon possible, massive catastrophe would affect us all! Would you survive?

And then there is that one predicted earthly catastrophe which will one day come, the end, the destruction of the entire sin-polluted creation, the last Day, Judgment Day, when the Lord will return to judge all people, before creating "a new heaven and a new earth, the home of righteousness" (2 Peter 3:13), which will never be corrupted by sin. Which seems impossible, since that promise was made so long ago, nearly 2000 years ago, but which is God's promise, so it will be – some day! Will you survive that catastrophe?

Well, everyone will survive it – in the sense of having a living existence! But will you survive it in the sense of having a life of blessing and joy or a continued existence of only misery?

Of course, we know the answer to that question of survival: we should experience only misery – that's what we sinners deserve! Every single one of us has lived in rebellion against God, even if only the rebellion of pride: I've done good, God! But there is so much more of our rebellion, yes, also by us who trust in Jesus as our Savior! Sure, we try to do what He says is good and right, but sometimes "my way" just seems better, so we do that in spite of what He says! Guilty! You and me – and everyone: guilty! So eternal misery, hell, is what we deserve!

But in His grace, His love for us helpless and hopeless sinners, God has acted to rescue us from eternal catastrophe. He did this, as we know, by entering our sinful existence to live without ever being even tainted by sin, but to be punished for sin, our sin. In His wisdom God focused all His anger against sin on that One Person hanging on that middle cross on that little hill outside Jerusalem. There He punished that One Person, Who, being also God – which is where God's plan becomes incomprehensible to our limited human understanding, for how can God punish God? – could and also did endure all the punishment all the sinning deserved, so that now "whoever believes in Him shall not perish but have eternal life" (John 3:16), such "believing" being not merely the bored "yes" of "o.k., it's true", but the committed trust of "no hope for me except what Jesus has done"!

But that eternal survival is different, isn't it? What I want to know is: will I survive any catastrophe which might come upon me in this life? But that cannot be known! Paul and those 275 others on that doomed ship knew, because God specifically promised survival to Paul, since God had special work for Paul yet to do. But us? If we should be in catastrophe and we should survive, then we also would know that He has a purpose for our continued living in this life, even if we should be disabled in some way. But if we do not survive, then we will know that this was His way of calling us into His eternal blessings.

Well, then, what good is it to even ask the question about survival? It is a reminder to us that we who trust in Jesus as our Savior are in God's hands, in His loving plan. Which is why we can have courage no matter what comes in this life, catastrophe or lesser troubles or even little difficulty at all (for some few do seem to have very few troubles to endure). He has promised to be with us whatever comes and to bring us through that, whether for continued living on earth with work to do for Him or to take us into eternal life, where we also will serve Him, but without any stain of sin.

What will come in life? Can't know! But we do know Who will be with us to take care of us. And so we will have courage to face and endure whatever will come!

January 26, 2014

Theme: **Your Future**

Related Reading: Luke 2:41-52

Text: 1 Samuel 16:1-13

HIS PLAN FOR YOUR LIFE

And so, what do you plan to do with your life? And, no, I haven't forgotten that most of you receiving this "Message" originally are pretty well set in life or coming closer to the end of your earthly life. So why ask what you plan to do with your life? That's a question usually asked of young people.

However, that saying about "where there's life, there's hope" can be validly amended to: "where there's life, there's purpose". For God does have a purpose for our still having life on earth. Whether one is very energetic or is slowed down by "Sir Arthur Itis" or even confined to home or bed, God still has a purpose for us here, before He calls us to be with Him there in eternity. And we need to realize that purpose, not only to carry it out better, but also to be defended against the ravaging attacks of despair – or boredom!

Our text tells us how a young man, probably a teenager, learned about God's plan for his life. The young man was David, so young and so little respected in his family that when the priest Samuel invited his family to a special sacrifice, Papa Jesse didn't include him, but sent him out to herd the sheep flock. After all, if the priest had a job for one of his sons, why Eliab was quite a man, apparently good looking and tall, so much so that Samuel even thought: "Surely the Lord's anointed stands here before the Lord." And if not Eliab, well, Abinadab was Papa Jesse's next favorite, and then Shammah and then four more of his sons. But none of them met God's standards, for, as the Lord told Samuel: "Man looks at the outward appearance, but the Lord looks at the heart."   So, seven sons and seven rejections!

"Are these all the sons you have", Papa Jesse? Because the Lord sent me here to select someone for a special purpose. Well, there is the kid, David, "but he is tending the sheep", too young to be of much more value than that. "Send for him," Samuel commanded; "we will not sit down (for this sacrifice feast) until he arrives." So David came – and he was the one! God had a special plan for his life – to be the next king over Israel.

David, though young, was a good-looking kid. But more importantly, the Lord knew he had a good-looking heart, a heart that took his faith seriously, that had the desire to live as faithfully as he could for the Lord. So the Lord told Samuel: "Rise and anoint him; he is the one." And from that moment on David realized God's plan for his life: to eventually replace Saul as king in order to lead the nation of Israel in faithfulness to the Lord. It all took a while, of course, but "from that day on the Spirit of the Lord came upon David in power."

And David did finally become the king and did serve faithfully – well, most of the time, that is, for his heart did get misled at times, most notably when his eyes saw Bathsheba taking a bath. But he repented, came back to faithfulness, and carried out God's plan of leading Israel to be God's nation on earth – at that time.

David was specifically blessed, of course, by being told what God's plan for him was. No such specific blessing for us. Some Christians claim that God does directly speak to them to guide them. And although occasionally such "guidance" does seem to work out well for the good of God's work on earth, still it is quite chancy, because too easily our sinful nature influences such "guidance" toward pride or selfishness or lust for possessions or power. So we have to be very careful about trusting our own impulses.

Instead, we need to sensibly evaluate the situation we are in and then think about what good we might be able to do in our situation, since God's basic guidance for all of His people is to do good – as His Word says: "For we are God's workmanship, created in Christ Jesus to do good works, which God prepared in advance for us to do" (Ephesians 2:10) – and did you notice God's plan in that verse? "Prepared in advance for us to do" – He has a plan for us in our lives, no matter at what stage in life we are now in. Another relevant verse is what Paul commanded Timothy to preach: "Command those who are rich in this present world...to put their hope in God...Command them to do good, to be rich in good deeds, and to be generous and willing to share" (1 Timothy 6:17-18). We all are "rich" by comparison to truly poor people in so much of the world. What is more, God's Word continually points all of His people to do what is good, what is helpful to others. That is, therefore, always His plan for your life and mine in the years or months or perhaps only weeks we still have in this life: to do good.

Which sometimes does not require much planning at all on our part. We can see the need of someone, the actual need, if we are looking for it. Yet even then it may take some evaluating. As example: should you automatically give something to someone holding a 'help me" sign at the side of the street? Have to be careful, because many such "needy" people make a good living by panhandling, while many others just want money to feed, not their stomachs, but their addictions. Same with appeals through the mail or over television: many use up most of the "help" in "administrative expenses" (translated: big salaries and expense accounts). Have to be careful. But also have to be willing to help where need is obvious and the helping will be truly helping for good.

Doing good applies not only toward other people, but also in one's own family: spouse, children, grandchildren, other relatives. Often this good is not so much connected with physical helping as it is with time, giving time to listen and to counsel or to understand even how one's own actions might be troubling others, then acting so harmony can be achieved or improved. Perhaps it is God's specific plan that we will be able to comfort or guide someone in our extended family by giving time to listen, to share tears as well as smiles, understanding and also encouragement. Of course, giving time to listen can be a "good" toward others we contact outside the family, too.

Sometimes the good we might do might open up other opportunities that have a wider application. Example: one man's love of singing eventually led to an active Community Chorus which gave much good to the singers involved and their audiences. Also, isn't it true that even large projects have to begin with an idea from just one person who saw a need, acted on it, then involved more people in doing that good? Which means that perhaps the Lord plans to use you in a wider good.

But most of us will never gain public recognition for the good we do, the little things of good which remain "little". And some of us (for I will also eventually enter this condition) may think: but what can I do of good – since I'm so limited in energy or ability or opportunity? Yes, if you are or will be in a nursing home, for example, what good can you do? Smile, pleasant conversation with the workers or other residents (if your hearing aids work adequately, of course), praying for others, speaking about Jesus to others – there always are opportunities for doing good – if we look for them no matter how active or limited we might be. And those opportunities are His plan for our life.

For He has looked at our hearts and knows that we do want to serve Him. Not that this was your or my original desire. By nature we want to serve ourselves and have others serve us. Which still is an attitude lurking in us, which sometimes we give in to, such as every time we sin. But He has come to us through His Word, specifically His good news of the good Jesus has done for us. And through that good news He has entered into our hearts, first to cause us to trust in what Jesus did, and then, to make us willing and able and wanting to do what He commands. Remember the passage mentioned a few minutes ago? "We are God's workmanship, created in Christ Jesus to do good works." So has He worked in us to be able to follow His plan for our lives – and to want to.

However, we don't always! All too often we let that lurking "serve me" desire take control – at least for a while. But then we hear and think again: God has "news" for us, the unexpected, the otherwise unknown, that Jesus knew this would keep happening, that we would always need the good He did for us, which is, first of all, that He lived perfectly for us, since we can't, and then the rest of God's plan that He has already paid the penalty for our failures, for all our sinning. That's what the "good news" of Baptism is: I've washed you clean by My shed blood. That's what the "good news" of Holy Communion is: yes, I did this "for you"!

What a relief! What a comfort! And also what a power! Because of the good He did for us, we now can want to do good to others and so will keep trying to follow His plan for our lives day by day. *January 13,*

Theme: **Giving**

Related Reading: 2 Corinthians 8:1-9

Text: 1 Peter 4:7-11

CAREFULLY MANAGING YOUR GIFTS

When I was still in the active ministry in charge of a congregation or two (and at times three or four), if a program came out from church headquarters about "Stewardship", automatically everyone knew it was an effort to get people to give more money. Sure, it paid "lip service" to the idea of the "stewardship" (wise management) of one's "time" and "talents", but it always ended up with emphasis on "treasure". One national president even was so crass as to say about money: "You've got it – we need it – so give it!"

I don't remember if I ever used any of those programs (except for specific fund-raising efforts for designated purposes), although there was a time or two when the congregation I served employed a professional fund-raising organization because of a major building project – however, I was reluctant about that. In contrast, rather than often preaching about money (or listing in the weekly bulletin what was given and what was needed each week – which is actually a form of preaching about money in my opinion), I followed the advice of a pastor I served under in the summer of 1955 in Wheaton, MN. Pastor Dierks explained his method of preaching about church finances: I preach about giving once a year to explain percentage giving – the rest of the year I bring people to the foot of the cross, and they bring their wallets with them. And it worked! His congregations didn't have any money problems. Because he was following Scripture! The power for giving to God through the church is not found in repeatedly preaching about giving – the power is the Gospel, the good news of Jesus being our Savior. As we consciously appreciate this, we do thank God with our voices and with our lives and with our dollars.

That is why in my preaching plan I focused on giving only once a year – to explain again God's plan of percentage giving: first decide what would be a percentage which would honor and thank God. Ten percent was an Old Testament law (which was increased by the animal sacrifices required to perhaps thirty percent!), but the New Testament never is that specific. All God's Word says in our new covenant time is (1 Corinthians 16:2): "Each one of you should set aside a sum of money *in keeping with his income*"; which means: first decide on the percentage, then apply it to your income (some Christians use their gross income amount, others their adjusted gross income, others whatever their checks amount to) and give from that. When the motive is: Jesus, our Savior, then our giving is "thank you", not "supposed to", and probably surprises us how generous it amounts to – and how joyful we are in that giving, for the emphasis in our minds is "Jesus", not "money".

I saw how this worked well in the congregations I

served, because God blessed the giving. We always had to be very careful in how we as a congregation spent what was given, but we never really had a "money problem" when the congregation followed this "program".

Well, this is my annual "stewardship" message. But this text has very little to do with the "stewardship of treasure" (giving money) – it is primarily about the "stewardship of time and talents", especially how we use the particular spiritual gifts God has given to us, as we are in faith.

"The end of all things is near. Therefore..." begins our text. This is to be another motive for how we carefully manage the gifts God has given us in life here on earth. And that motive is the assurance that we will live beyond "life here on earth"! We will live forever! With God! Which we have no right to expect, because we aren't always careful in how we live, how we use our time or abilities – or money, too! Just the other day I told Marian: I hope to get at writing this week's "Message" soon this morning – if I don't "fritter away" too much time! (As it turned out, I "frittered" some, but not as much as sometimes and so was able to write this specific "Message" fairly quickly – could have been better, so I need forgiveness in this also, but it could have been much worse – which isn't self-righteous thinking, just stating the fact).

So, eternal life through Jesus is our motive for being good managers of all the gifts God gives us, because eternal life is also what He gives us: "the gift of God is eternal life"

(Romans 6:23). On what basis? This gift is "in Christ Jesus our Lord". Jesus and what He has done for us sinners, He is always our motive – so that we give thanks.

"The end of all things is near", but Peter recognized that it isn't coming very quickly. For he was inspired to write about how we are to live until then: "be clear-minded and self-controlled". We are not to act on the basis of emotions, but on the basis of facts: the fact of Jesus and the facts as we see them in life – not as they are "spun" by politicians (in these election days) or even by family or friends (meaning: everyone – even we ourselves – "spin" what we've done to put ourselves in the best light possible, especially if we've not done too well – "excuses" is what we call it, especially when we can blame something or someone else instead of taking personal responsibility). So, face life with clear thinking, which keeps our emotions under control (which is "easier said than done", of course, but this is to be our aim in how we live).

To do what? First thing Peter writes is: "so that you can pray". Turn to the Lord first – always! Doesn't have to take a lot of time – especially if action is required when there isn't much time to act. Still, one can always pray: Lord, help me in this situation! Please! But we have to be clear-minded and self-controlled to take that brief moment to remember to pray instead of just blindly act.

Next: "Above all, love each other deeply"; again, not as in feeling, but in acting to help according to what the other person really needs, especially if that person is so stirred up as to not really know what is good to do or get; example, "give me a drink" probably will only make things worse – or, a violent video game will not be good for a teenager no matter how much he or she "has to" have it.

"Love covers over a multitude of sins", writes Peter, which means that not only will we help in spite of how the person has sinned (even against us), but also that our helping might prevent further sinning from happening – and could lead the person to forgiveness of sins in Jesus.

"Offer hospitality to one another without grumbling" – this is the only thing in this text about stewardship that is directly connected to financial giving; but even this "hospitality" involves more the use of time than anything else. Yet it may cost a meal or more – with a good attitude, not grumbling about what else I could be doing instead. Which at times involves a bit of "self-control", given our sinful natures.

Then comes the specific direction to use the particular gifts the Lord gives us as His children by faith: "Each one should use whatever gift he has received to serve others, faithfully administering God's grace in its various forms". This may be verbally ("if anyone speaks") or physically ("if anyone serves"). We each have different abilities – and opportunities. God has called us to use these "so that in all things God may be praised through Jesus Christ".

"Speaking" may be preaching or teaching for some; but for all of us there are opportunities of speaking good to others (complimenting, encouraging) and speaking about Jesus as Savior (when the time seems right – this is also where that being "clear-minded and self-controlled" is important – because one just cannot speak of Jesus in every conversation or incident – but we can think of ways to guide a conversation so we can speak of Him – sometimes!).

And serving, that is, helping others – which is referring to the deeds of Christian love – "with the strength God provides", that is, He will help us do the good we are doing to help someone. And sometimes, as in our giving, even we will be surprised at how much we end up being able to do, because He has been strengthening us. Then when people thank us for helping, can't that give us at least a brief opportunity to bring Jesus into the conversation or relationship? Perhaps we can say: I'm glad you like what I've been able to do, but really Jesus is the One Who guided me to give you this help. Not each time, but sometimes this might be just the thing to say as we witness for Jesus, if we are "clear-minded" enough to think of it.

Overall, the Lord calls us to use our lives, until He returns, to praise Him so that in anything and everything we do, we are actually meaning: "To Him be the glory and the power forever and ever".

How blessed we are to receive His eternal blessing because of Jesus and to be a blessing to others as His servants. Which we will be, as we carefully use our time and our talents and, yes, also our treasures in this life, until we finally are with Him eternally.

November 2, 2014

Theme: **Witnessing**

Related Reading: Acts 11:19-26

Text: 1 Peter 2:4-10

ADVERTISING THE GOSPEL

Advertising! Everyone who runs a business knows you have to advertise, if your business is to succeed. Although the church has some business characteristics, the church is not a business. Yet, the church has to advertise, if it is even to survive. In fact, our text says we are supposed to advertise, not the church as such, but to advertise God and what He has done for sinners. The specific words of our text say in English translation: "You are a chosen people...that you may declare the praises of (God)" – translators usually say "declare", but the Greek word actually could be translated "advertise".

However, such advertising is not a matter of our now purchasing space on a billboard or a spot on TV. Instead, this advertising has already been purchased by God, specifically by God the Son, Jesus, "the living Stone", the "precious cornerstone", the "capstone", Who paid with His life, paid for us sinners. We are God's advertising in this sinful world – we are to be advertising what God has done, not only for us sinners, but for all sinners. We are to be advertising the Gospel, God's good news of forgiveness for sinners, His peace for sinners. This is our purpose for still living: to advertise the Gospel.

Usually we call this activity "witnessing", telling others about Jesus, Who came to be their Savior as well as ours. And so, preachers continually – and I have also – commanded us all: Witness! Tell your family, tell your friends, tell your neighbors!

But such commands overlook the reality for us who have come to faith in Jesus for our forgiveness and peace, the reality that it just isn't easy, no matter how much we know we should and even want to. And it's not really a matter of being afraid – although often we are. Nor is it a matter of ignorance on our part about what to say, for if we trust in Jesus, we can say that, can't we – which is all we are expected to say, since if it is good enough for me a sinner, it is good enough for any other sinner. Instead, it is difficult to find or to make an opportunity without seeming like we are somehow just forcing our ideas on an unsuspecting and unwilling victim.

As example: Marian and I live in a gated, 55+ community – very ordinary income level required (else we couldn't afford it). People are friendly, compatible – most of them. Many are Christians. But some are even outspoken in their rejection of spiritual matters. We want to witness to them, to share with them about Jesus. But how to do it – in a non-threatening and in a natural conversational way so they are willing listen? Sometimes opportunities do just happen – and sometimes the only way is to ask someone permission: could I talk to you about what is so important in my life? But it isn't easy – it doesn't happen that often. That's reality in my life; I suspect that's reality for you, too. So, what can we do?

That's it! We have to *do* something before we can *say* anything! Why else do Nutrisystem and Jenny Craig use real people with before and after photos and with "pounds lost" prominently displayed? Here's the proof, folks! You can see it! And since it worked for these people, it can work for you, too! Which means that our first form of advertising the Gospel is showing that it works! Showing in our lives that we can have peace, we can have courage, we can be kind and forgiving, we can be faithful, we can be honest, that we can be – that we are!

After all, if the Gospel hasn't made us any different as believers from unbelievers, why should an unbeliever bother with us and our words? In fact, if our lives do not show that we are following Jesus, are we following Him at all? Faith for forgiveness is not just a matter of words which pat us on the back and tell us we can keep on in that sinning with no change expected! No! Faith involves repentance! And repentance does not mean just saying – or even feeling: I'm sorry; repentance means turning away from that sinning with the plea: Lord, help me not to do this again!

"Help me not to do this again!" That's the key, the reality – for we cannot promise that we never will again – our human nature betrays us too easily. But we want to be different from the wrong we are guilty of, we want to do right, so: Lord, help me! Have mercy ! In fact, that's what mercy is: help!

Reality at this point also means that since our sinful human nature remains so strong, at times our plea is: Lord, help me want to want to do different, to do right!

When we do have that attitude of repentance, it is a struggle, but the Lord does gradually change us. Ask a recovering alcoholic or drug addict about the struggle! Ask someone who used to have an explosive anger but doesn't any more – well, not most of the time. The Holy Spirit does change us – gradually at least – so that others can see we are different than unbelievers in very good ways.

That repentant living, that daily effort to do what is right and good, that is the first and actually the most important advertising which we do: we show what God has done for us by showing what God is doing in our lives. Which is what Jesus said, isn't it? "Let your light shine...that they may see your good deeds" (Matthew 5:16). The more we show the Gospel's effect in us, the more we can further advertise the Gospel by what we say about Jesus.

The only way we can change and keep changing so we are good advertisements for God's good news, however, is as we keep receiving that good news ourselves. Yet not just in the same words week after week – I mean, God's good news is not merely repeating the words of John 3:16, "God so loved the world..." God's Word uses many different ways to explain what He has done for us so we think of it consciously and sincerely. If we only hear the very same words, then our human nature turns off our thinking, because: "I've heard that before, so I don't need to listen again."

Which is why in our text God inspired Peter to use a different way of illustrating and explaining His work of saving us. It's the picture of using stones to build a house with emphasis on the cornerstone and the capstone. In those days, as I understand it, builders would make sure that a building was square by first making a large rock perfectly square so they could then sight along it to keep the wall straight and true. Jesus is that spiritual cornerstone so that we see and know that the only way to eternal life is through what He did; and He gives us the straight way to live until we get there.

The capstone was that center stone in an arch which kept the arch entry in place – take it away and the arch collapsed. Take Jesus away from that straight way to eternal life, think He isn't essential because you aren't such a bad person, and the way collapses – and the sinner is crushed spiritually. Jesus is the only way – proud sinners who reject Him stumble and fall away from God forever.

Both illustrations are teaching us: keep awake, sinner, keep trusting only in Jesus, for He is the only One Who can save us.

As we hear and think about that reality, we will

continue to trust that fact, and the Lord will continue to work in us so that we will show other sinners that He makes a difference not only for eternity but also in this life. That advertising by deeds then makes it possible to advertise with our words when we do have or make the opportunity to speak of Jesus.

But the life advertising has to be evident first. Only then can the Holy Spirit use our words as His effective tools in others to bring them to faith also. And He will help us so to advertise, as we keep hearing God's good news: Jesus has bought you free from your sins so you can be His advertisement to others!

October 23, 2011

Related Reading: Romans 6:12-23

Text: Luke 11:24-26

TIME! NOT ENOUGH! TOO MUCH!

Undoubtedly you remember the old saying: "Idle hands are the devil's workshop". Some of you, hurried and harried by the pressure of life, might woefully respond: Who's got time to be idle? And others of you, perhaps retired or shut-in or just drifting in your particular circumstances, might respond wistfully: I've got too much time on my hands! Time! We all have the same amount each day: 24 hours – 1440 minutes – 86,400 seconds – in what we call a "day". We have that time, each of us. The question is: what do we do with all those daily seconds? Which is what Jesus is actually warning about in our text.

From the New Testament we know that possession of a person, that is, strict control of that person, by an evil spirit, one of the devil's workers, is quite real. Skeptics today dismiss the very idea as merely the superstition of ignorant people back then. But if Scripture says it, it must be so. And perhaps there is more evil spirit possession today than even we who believe God's Word are ready to admit. Because when we see evidence of utter ruthless disregard for human life, when some people so cruelly torture helpless people, when some individuals continually repeat self-destructive actions, one has to wonder if that might be "demon possession".

One fact which comforts us who trust in Jesus as Savior, however, is that we cannot be possessed, totally controlled by an evil spirit, because as John wrote (I,4:4): "the One Who is in you is greater than the one who is in the world". However, we do have to be on guard and struggle against the devil's attacks through his evil spirits, because God's Word would not warn us (1 Peter 5:8) that the devil "prowls around like a roaring lion looking for someone to devour", if it were not so. Therefore, any Christian can lose his or her faith – and then possibly become "possessed by a devil" – it is a danger. And, of course, we face the daily, no, the second-by-second danger of temptation, which is the devil's initial attack.

Jesus is warning us of that in this text. He was speaking directly about those whom He had freed from evil spirit possession: When you have been set free, you are not out of the woods of spiritual danger – you have to fill up your time with the good God commands or your relapse will be worse than the initial problem; you cannot live in a spiritual vacuum – either you let God's Spirit work in you more and more or the devil will take over again! So warned Jesus!

Think of drug addiction as an illustration. If a person has made the effort to "dry out", "kick the habit", that person cannot just drift. That person has to use the support system of learning about his or her emotional and spiritual problems and especially use the personal help of true friends – not so-called "friends" who have their own addictions. Otherwise, that person will soon fall back into worse addiction – Whitney Houston being a recent public example – how sad – so much talent – and no one truly gave her the help she needed.

But we are not – at least I pray that none of you are – caught up in addiction or, worse, struggling with the devil seemingly about to take control of your life. If you are, take heart! Be encouraged! Jesus will help you in your struggle! He does it through the power of His good news, His good news for you! Yes, for you, no matter what you have done, even have just been doing! He did not come to rescue good people, winners; He came to rescue losers – which includes all of us, because to sin is to lose – and all of us lose somewhat every day. And it did not matter to Jesus, as He entered this world of time, how "lost" a person is.

In the "March Madness" of NCAA basketball it doesn't matter if you lose by one point or by a hundred – if you lose, you are done, lost! So Jesus came for all of us "losers". He accepted responsibility for all of us – He played the perfect "game" in order to change us from sinful "losers" into spiritual "winners"! And He did it for you no matter how guilty you feel, just as I am included, as guilty as I am. We humans want to approach God by comparison: No, pastor, surely you haven't done what I've done, so you are not as guilty! But God's justice knows no degrees of guilt: either "guilty" or "not guilty" – we can stay in our guilt or we can allow Him to pronounce us as "not guilty", not by error in His judgment, but because of what Jesus did – for you, guilty one – for me, guilty one. That is God's good new!

That is our comfort – as we believe it.

Which brings us back to this thing we call "time", these moments which make up the days of living. What will we do with our time? As we trust Jesus for our "not guilty" judgment, what will we do as we now live? Whether we never seem to have enough time, because we are so crowded by unavoidable responsibilities, or whether we do have time on our hands, how will we use the time God is giving us day by day? Different answers for each of us, of course, different if your time is "booked solid", different if you truly don't have enough to do. But let's think about possibilities.

The key use of our time is to be helping others. And if you should now react: But I don't have enough time to get everything done already that I have to do at my job, for my family, so how can I add more? – the answer is: not more quantity of deeds, but quality in what you are doing! For what is your job? Merely drudgery to get a paycheck? Or merely taking care of the family? If so, no wonder you are so frustrated! But if you see your work as your contribution in helping accomplish something good for people – especially in your family, then you will have satisfaction in knowing that this is how you are serving God in a special way: you are helping others.

Serving God, we must realize, is not primarily or only when we are doing something at or for the church. Nor is it "really serving God" even if we take time to go on a church mission trip or to help at a "soup kitchen". True "church work" is our daily work – as we help people in the community (as ordinary as a checker at the grocery store perhaps) or in our family (folding the clothes, helping the kids with homework or just talking with your spouse) or talking with friends, too – this is truly serving God as He desires. So, if you are truly too busy to do anything special, remember to do what you are doing as helping others; that is using time as our Lord desires, that is showing faith in Jesus for having rescued you from being an eternal "loser" to being on His "winning" team! If you look at your work without that attitude of: this is how I help others and so serve my Savior God, then you will get not only bored, but could drift into over-tired rebellion and eventually fall back into being a "loser", because you will have lost your faith. But keep Jesus as "winner" in mind and that you are on His winning team, and He will keep you safe, for you will keep on listening to His Word in order to follow Him in your daily allotment of time.

And for those of us who do have more time than responsibilities, we need to make the conscious effort to use our time, not just "kill" it. How easy it can be – and how unsatisfying also – just to stare at the TV or diddle with the smart phone or play meaningless computer games (as I know from too much experience). Instead, we need to evaluate our day: what can I do today that is worthwhile, that is helpful to someone. It is not wrong or sinful to spend some of our time in recreation – God knew His creatures would need rest and relaxation and so set up the weekly pattern of a day of "rest". But He does not give us all the time of a day just to play. He gives us time so we can he helpful to others in some way.

Yes, even if you are limited in what you can do, because your body is wearing out! How you talk with the people you are in contact with can be nasty and hurtful and self-pitying or it can be helpful and kind – such helpful talk may not take up all your time, but it is something at least. And there can be letters to write and prayers to be prayed for others and telephone calls to make. Or, maybe you aren't totally limited so you could be able to volunteer in a helpful way. It is good to ask yourself: what helping thing can I do today? And then be alert to try to help by word or deed, as God allows opportunities to become available.

Obviously, this looking to see how to be helpful will not fill up all of your time – if you have too much extra time; nor will it remove all stress from your hurried life – if you don't seem to have enough time. But it will bring you the blessing of knowing that you are trying to do His will on earth as you travel through time on your way to eternal life, which you are thankful for, since it is His gift to you because of Jesus.

March 25, 2012

Theme: **Forever**

Related Reading: Revelation 21:1-8

Text: John 5:24-30

FOREVER AND EVER AND EVER

A question – be careful how you answer it: How long are you going to live? Your immediate response most likely is: Don't know – no one can know how long they will live! But you are wrong to think that – because everyone is going to live the same length of life. What? Impossible! Yet true! There was a little tract many, many years ago which gave the answer: "You are going to live forever – like it or not!" Because that's what the Bible teaches, in fact, that's what we confess in the Apostles' Creed: "the life everlasting". Once a person has begun to exist, to live, from that first moment of sperm entering ovum, that person will live forever and ever and ever. We each have an undying personality, which we typically call "the soul", but which actually is you yourself, your personal awareness of yourself apart from the touchable part of you, which is your body. And you, I, we will live forever and ever and ever.

Now, of course, how long we will live in our bodies on this earth does vary for each of us, and we don't know our length of life on this earth – and, please note, I specifically am referring to "this" earth. The psalm (Psalm 90:10) says: "three score years and ten", that is, 70 years, or maybe "four score years", 80, has been typical for most of history in most places – that is, for those who survived early childhood death or warfare. And now many, many of us Americans are living 90, even 100 years, and more; in fact, nearly 100,000 Americans are centenarians and over 300,000 are 100 or more world-wide. How long will you or I live on this earth? Only the Lord knows.

And after this life, the next life? That's the life in heaven, in Paradise, as Jesus told the criminal on the cross; how long will you live in heaven, that is, without your body, if you make it into heaven, of course, which is part of Jesus' teaching in our text – which we will get to momentarily – after we answer: how long will we live in heaven? Again, we might automatically answer: Forever and ever and ever – for that's what we assume when we think of having eternal life with Jesus. But that answer is wrong! No one will live in heaven, that is, in the paradise of being in God's presence without one's body, no one will live there forever and ever and ever! Instead, Jesus in our text teaches there will be a day "when all who are in their graves will hear His voice and come out" – that day being the Last Day, Judgment Day, the day of the resurrection of our bodies! That day we will be re-united with our bodies to be whole again, as whole touchable persons! So, we will live in heaven from the moment we die physically and leave our bodies to decay, until God re-creates our bodies to give them back to us in "the resurrection of the body", as the creed says, because that's what the Bible teaches in: our text, in Job 19, Matthew 25, 1 Corinthians 15, and 1 Thessalonians 4 to refer to only a few places in Scripture which clearly teach this.

And then? How long will we live in our resurrected bodies? Now finally the correct answer is: Forever and ever and ever! That is "the life everlasting", which will be not on this earth, but on the re-created earth, the new creation, the new universe, which we will witness God creating on the Last Day, that Resurrection-of-the-Body Day, when first He will completely destroy the present universe to make a new universe which will last forever and ever and ever, but never, never ever be contaminated by sin as this earth is! This is God's promise to us (2 Peter 3): the life everlasting, His kingdom which shall have no end.

At this point we have to backtrack into our text, because with that kind of a future ahead of us, how can we be sure we will be part of it and not outside of His kingdom which will have no end? Jesus teaches how very specifically in our text: "I tell you the truth: whoever hears My word and believes Him Who sent Me has eternal life and will not be condemned; he has crossed over from death to life. I tell you the truth: a time is coming and now has come when the dead will hear the voice of the Son of God and those who hear (that is, the hearing of faith, not merely sounds vibrating on one's eardrums) – those who hear will live."

Jesus says here as well as throughout the entire Bible: everyone should be condemned, because everyone sins – everyone has failed God's requirement of perfection. But people then were beginning to hear His message and would soon hear His full message that He is the one through Whom sinners are rescued from condemnation and separation from the holy and only God.

We, of course, have it easier to understand and believe this, because we have it all written out for us to personally read in the Bible, the good news that: Jesus was not merely a human being, but was God come to earth – Jesus was not a sinner like very other human being, but was perfect in all He did so that He could save sinners – Jesus was not executed by crucifixion according to Roman justice as the two criminals that day with Him, but was actually put on that cross by the plan of God so He could be punished according to God's justice for the sins of everyone so that "everyone who believes in Him shall not perish but have eternal life" (John 3:16). That is the message to be heard, the message from God Himself, which, when we believe it, that is, when we personally trust Jesus did this for me, this message rescues us from our spiritual deadness in sin and from the condemnation we deserve.

This, by the way, is called in Revelation 20 "the first resurrection" – with its benefit, says Revelation 20 (sounding very similar to our text): "Blessed and holy are those who have part in the first resurrection – the second death (that is, the death of condemnation forever) has no power over them" (vv.5-6). So, if you are trusting in Jesus as your Savior right now – and remain in this faith, of course – you can look forward to: a. life in heaven, in Paradise, immediately when you die, and, b. "the resurrection of the body and the life everlasting" on and after Judgment Day. Before faith we were spiritually dead; now the Holy Spirit, by bringing us to faith, has given us life, real life for and with God.

Have to explain one more part of our text; Jesus says: "A time is coming when all who are in the graves will hear His voice and come out (that is, the resurrection of the body event – all, believers and unbelievers, will get their bodies back – but then the part requiring explanation), those who have done good will rise to live, and those who have done evil will rise to be condemned" – which sounds like, doesn't it, that in the end we will be judged by what we do, not by faith in Jesus – which the description in Matthew 25 (vv.34-40) also sounds like, when Jesus says: "Come, you who are blessed by My Father, take your inheritance...For I was hungry and you gave Me something to eat...thirsty...stranger...naked...sick...in prison and you (helped)"-- never a word about faith, so, do we earn "the life everlasting" by the good we do, after all?

Not at all, for sin cannot be made up for by us sinners. Instead, the only sinners who can do what God judges as "good" are those sinners who "believe Him" (Jesus), that is, who are trusting in what He did, not what they do. Without this faith we cannot do anything good in His judgment – we just sin. But in faith we show that we are trusting in Jesus by doing what is right and good and kind and helpful, as we have opportunity in our daily living.

So, in summary: you and I, as we are trusting in Jesus, will live forever – in this body on this earth for a limited time – without our bodies in heaven until Judgment Day – then in our re-created bodies on the re-created earth in His eternal kingdom – which means, of course, that, if He will be king, we will somehow be obeying Him, not merely singing either, but living, doing, helping.

And until then, in this life, because we are thankful for this life to come forever and ever and ever, we will try to do day by day, not what is sinning, but what is right and good and kind and helping, for this is how we now glorify our Father in heaven and Jesus, His Son, our Savior.

November 14, 2010

Theme: **Now**

Related Reading: 1 Thessalonians 5:1-11

Text: 2 Timothy 3:1-9

THE LAST DAYS??

Oh, boy! Could there be a better description of current American culture than our text? Just read it again: "People will be lovers of themselves, lovers of money, boastful, proud, abusive..." and all the rest including even the many false "evangelists" on television who "worm their way into homes and gain control over weak-willed women (and men as well) who are loaded down with sins and are swayed by all kinds of evil desires", etc. Surely Paul was unknowingly writing about us, right? So, we surely must be in "the last days" and Jesus will come, definitely within our life-times, right?

Except! The early Christians expected Jesus to return in their life-times! As Paul wrote to the Thessalonians: "we who are still alive, who are left till the coming of the Lord" (I,4:15). And some of these Thessalonians had heard teaching that "the Lord has already come" (II,2:2). They were mistaken, as the apostle quickly instructed them (2 Thessalonians II,2:1-2). However, they had human reason to expect the possibility of the last day then already, because Jesus Himself said about all the predicted warning signs: "I tell you the truth, this generation will certainly not pass away until all these things have happened" (Matthew 24:34), which means: at least some of those living, as He spoke, would be alive while all the signs would have taken place.

As they have been repeatedly fulfilled ever since so that some Christians have been absolutely convinced that the last days were almost *right* **now**! Example, the followers of the "Millerite movement", which eventually gave birth to the Seventh Day Adventist Church, were so convinced that Jesus would return on October 22, 1844, that thousands stayed up all night out in the hills to see Him come!

Of course, they were wrong – not, however, about all the signs having been fulfilled, but about when Jesus would return.. And what did Jesus teach about "when"? "No one knows about that day or hour, not even the angels in heaven, nor the Son (according to His human nature on earth as He was speaking has to be His meaning), but only the Father" (Matthew 24:36). And Peter warned: "The day of the Lord will come like a thief" (II,3:10) – totally unexpectedly!

Which means that our contemporary culture with all its evils is just another fulfillment of this sign which has been fulfilled repeatedly in past history. Even in our country! For is our culture today significantly different from the Prohibition years with all its violence built on the lust of people to "have a good time"? And the religious misleading of people, such as the Millerites referred to a bit ago; how about the blatant unChristianity of Norman Vincent Peale and Robert Schuller, both of whom had tremendous followings, but neither of whom proclaimed Jesus as the only Savior – yet they sure raked in tons of money in support. Sorry, folks – our current primarily evil culture is not an at-last-indication that Jesus will return for us to see! Since the signs have all been fulfilled repeatedly, could be! But not definitely! Because Jesus taught: unexpectedly!

Yet, not "unexpectedly" as though no one cares if or when. We are to look forward to His return – and to live faithfully, because He is returning. This is what Peter writes: "What kind of people ought you to be? You ought to live holy and godly lives as you look forward to the day of God...So then, dear friends, since you are looking forward to this, make every effort to be found spotless, blameless, and at peace with Him" (II,3:11-12,14).

Still, that is not our real motive for faithfulness, is it? Expecting His return is a motive added to our thanks for His work while on earth during His lifetime and His death-time so we can look forward to His return with joy and peace instead of with fear and dread. Our primary motive is what He has already done, not what He still will do. That is what makes us able to and want to live His way. Because the Lord God has already judged us to be righteous in His sight..

When He looks at our cases in His eternal court, He should judge us all: Guilty! Unrighteous! Condemned! For that is what our sins have earned! But then our "defense lawyer" (1 John 2:1), Jesus, "speaks to the Father on our behalf" and says: True! They did it, Father. But remember: You laid their guilt upon Me – You made Me "Who had no sin to be sin for (them) so that (they would) become the righteousness" which Your justice demands (2 Corinthians 5:21). and so, looking at this evidence – the cross as evidence, the eternal Judge pronounces His verdict: For those who are hiding behind what You, My Son, have done: Righteous! Not guilty! Forgiven!

In stubborn pride, however, most sinners reject this way of God! What a miscarriage of justice, they in effect say. No matter what Jesus did, I demand that You judge me on the basis of what I have done or on the basis of how sorry I am! Give me justice!

To which the Judge has no reply except: Guilty! Condemned forever – to get what you deserve for sinning.

You, however, I trust, as well as I, have taken "the Way" offered by Jesus, right? Thank you, Jesus, that You have defended us so that we look forward to Your return with joy and anticipation.

And, therefore, He is why we live as faithfully as we can – well, to be stone cold sober about it, we try to. Because our sinful nature keeps us from living even as faithfully as we could live – we still are tempted – and we still give in somewhat from time to time (although truthfully, daily, correct?). Which makes us even more thankful for what He has done for us sinners – that He has hidden also these daily sins from the Judge's eyes.

Yet, He wants us, He expects us to resist the ways of this

ungodly world ("world" being the people, not the creation) such as are listed in our text. Paul writes that these ways of ungodly living will become more and more prevalent. He is not only predicting – he is warning – in effect saying: this is the world you will live in – and so many will be living this way and apparently enjoying it so much (to all appearances, it must be added) that you will be greatly tempted to do the same. Don't! For these are the ways of unbelief!

Did Paul really mean what I'm saying here? Yes, because just a few verses before our text he had written: "Flee the evil desires of youth" – which desires are not only lust and greed, but also ambition, "my way", excitement, and outward show to cover up inner ugliness and selfishness. Our text, then, is giving specific examples of these "evil desires of youth", because unbelievers never grow up – they can't! They are stuck in their sinful natures with no ability to be really different.

True, there are some apparently "good" and "mature" people. But the world as a whole, the increasing culture which we see, is dead and deadly – unless a person has an eyes-wide-open faith in Jesus, which recognizes the evils and turns instead to, as Paul wrote in those previous verses, "pursue righteousness, faith, love and peace". And these are not instructions only for a pastor, which Timothy was, but for each of us who trust in and follow Jesus.

Are we in the very last days of this corrupted creation? Could be – but we can't say. So we are not to live with a constant thought: Will today be the last day? (Just as someone with so many years piling up can not live with the constant thought: Will this be the day I die?) Instead, aware of the last day coming (or of our own personal last day), we greet each day with joyful thanks: *Thank You, Lord, for this day – please help me live it in faithfulness to You and the way You want me to live. Amen.*

November 16, 2014

Theme: **A Caution**

Related Reading: 2 Timothy 3:16-18

Text: 1 Peter 5:6-11

WHEN THE LION ROARS

Have you ever heard a lion roar? Not the MGM lion nor one in a zoo, but a real one – out in the wild? Most likely not, nor I. But it's rather easy to imagine the fear that blood-curdling roar might cause. Yet that fear would be unfounded – at least about that particular lion. For a lion doesn't roar when it is stalking its prey, because that would scare his next meal off. Nor does it roar, the experts say, after having made a kill. No, when a lion roars, it's because he is reminding all the other lions – and other animals – around that this is his territory – and his "pride" of lionesses and younger lions. In effect the male lion is saying: Don't mess with me! I'm boss! So in reality one doesn't have to fear that distant lion. He's not prowling for you now.

Still, there is cause to fear – or at least be uneasy. For if the boss lion is within hearing distance, then there are other lions around, perhaps nearby; and they could be on the prowl for you, so you had better be alert – and careful.

In our world today one could say that the lion is sure roaring in distant countries – with Christians especially in danger. For all this killing of Christians by Muslims (the "politically correct" people say they shouldn't be called "Muslim", "because they've hijacked" the Muslim beliefs;

316

but the truth is that they are truly acting on their beliefs as taught in the Koran about killing "infidels" – which often also includes other Muslims, yet especially targeting Christians and Jews), all this barbaric behavior is a result of the devil's tempting and controlling. Yet, it truly is "far away" – at least for now – so, we don't have to be afraid of facing that kind of death – not yet anyway – although that "not yet" can cause us some uneasiness perhaps: Would I be "faithful unto death" (Revelation 2:10), as so many brothers and sisters in faith around the world are proving to be today? But I don't have to be concerned about that right now – it is so distant.

However, the distant roar must remind us that less vocal "lions" are prowling around much closer, "looking for someone to devour": stealthily trying to destroy our faith. For faith can be quickly lost, even unaware that it is happening, as we live in the culture of our everyday world with all its greed and violence and immorality and examples of revenge and hate, each of which involves a killing of faith, when one gives in to their lure.

These cultural facts can become truly alluring. We can see and hear so much of it via news reports and entertainment that we can begin to be less and less troubled by these evils to the point of finally accepting them as ordinary without realizing their destructiveness or, more likely, denying their deadliness. I mean: of course you have to have alcohol or drugs to have a good party – of course you have to dress in current styles even though they are provocative – of course you have to get revenge else others will get away with taking advantage of you – of course you have to buy and buy more things and more excitement to have a happy life – and of course you can never forgive someone who has deeply hurt you – of course!

However, God's Word says that these are the ways of death, of unbelief! To give in to them is to be "devoured"! We may not have to be too concerned about death by beheading. But because of nearby dangers we surely need to "be self-controlled and alert" so we will not give in and go along with unbelieving ways, but will "resist" and "stand firm in the faith". In a sense, we need a bit of spiritual fear in our lives, an awareness that we could be "devoured", could lose our faith.

Peter was inspired to warn his readers – those back then and us right now – about the spiritual danger threatening anyone who trusts in and follows Jesus. We dare not take our faith for granted, as though we are absolutely safe, never in danger. No matter how faithful we have been, God here tells us: "Be self-controlled and alert"! There is danger!

Not only is danger possible, but damage will be inflicted! God's Word is not idealistic in the sense that once a person has come to faith, spiritual life will just flow easily. Oh, no! Physical suffering can easily cause spiritual damage, and living in an evil culture often takes a toll on one's faith. This is why very realistically Peter writes: "After you have suffered a little while, (God) will Himself restore you and make you strong, firm and steadfast". This is a picture of repairing a house damaged by a violent storm or flooding: the house is still standing but there are holes to be patched and walls to be braced and the roof to be reshingled and the foundation to be repaired. So does God recognize that our individual house of faith can and does get damaged, even when it does not totally collapse.

When Satan's cohorts attack, we sometimes do give in a bit: our angry words can hurt, our hurt feelings can make us think revenge or not want to forgive, our thoughts can flirt with immorality or greed, and we can do things which are flat out wrong! That happens – so easily! And sometimes the "house of faith" can even "collapse": faith can be lost!

But our God does not turn away from us in disgust. He should! Think how Jesus gave Himself for all our sins – suffered more than we could ever stand! And we don't appreciate His sacrifice enough to keep away from these sins and evils in order to "stand firm in the faith"! Why should God still put up with us, still care about us, still rescue us?

But He does! He promises in this text especially that He "will Himself restore you and make you strong, firm and steadfast"! He promises to forgive us, as well as help us return to faithfulness.

Yet, all of this can give us some anxiety, spiritual anxiety – because of the "what ifs". What if it gets to be too much for me? What if I'm not "faithful unto death"? What if He tries to bring me back but I don't respond – because I feel too damaged, too guilty? What if! Anxiety!

Could that be precisely why the Holy Spirit inspired Peter to write: "Cast all your anxiety upon Him, because He cares for you"? We do not know, we cannot know, what may come, what may attack, what we might have to experience. And sometimes we begin to wonder, to worry, to be fearful. It may be about the spiritual struggles we just have been thinking about these past few minutes in this "Message". Or it may be about the physical trials which may be coming, especially as the "golden years" lose their luster as one's body doesn't even seem like silver any more but more like lead, and one wonders what physical suffering might still be ahead. Or it may be about how you are going to manage to survive into those so-called "golden years", given the troubles you fear might be coming in this deteriorating culture we live in. Many sources of anxiety, many kinds of anxiety.

So God says: Give them to Me! Let Me take care of you, no matter what comes. I have My hand over you to protect and guide you. Yes, how and where I lead you may not be easy. But trust Me! I surely will "lift you up in due time" – I will "restore you and make you strong, firm and steadfast". Of course, you need to "be self-controlled and alert" – you need to be keeping close to Me through My Word proclaimed to you in worship and given to you in Holy Communion – "keeping close" meaning: not merely observing rituals but "self-controlled and alert" to receive the help I give.

Which is why we can have peace now, no matter what will come. Life has suffering, all because of sin, our sinning, others sinning. But that suffering will be only for "a little while". And since He will help us, we can leave our anxieties in His hands and instead focus on how we can best honor Him by how we live today – and each day that comes.

March 8, 2015

ABOUT THE AUTHOR

Theodore Allwardt is a retired Lutheran pastor,
who served congregations in North Dakota,
Missouri, Idaho, New Mexico, and Oregon.
Many of his "Messages from the Coast"
have been published in *Christian News*.
He has also written:
Rattlesnakes and Rainbows:
Daily Devotions Along the Trail of Life.
He and his wife, Marian, have
three children and six grandchildren;
they live in Brookings, OR.

Made in the USA
Charleston, SC
25 November 2015